Louis I. Kahn

LIGHT AND SPACE

Louis I. Kahn

LIGHT AND SPACE

Urs Büttiker

WHITNEY LIBRARY OF DESIGN

an imprint of Watson-Guptill Publications/New York

Translation: David Bean

Copyright © 1994 by Birkhäuser Verlag

First published in the United States in 1994 by Whitney Library of Design,
an imprint of Watson-Guptill Publications, a division of BPI Communications, Inc.,
1515 Broadway, New York, NY 10036.

Library of Congress Cataloging-in-Publication Data

Büttiker, Urs, 1952-
   Louis I. Kahn : light and space / Urs Büttiker.
     p. cm.
   Previously published in a bilingual English/German ed., Basel :
 Boston : Birkhäuser Verlag, c1993.
  Includes bibliographical references (p. 182).
  ISBN 8230-2773-2 HC   ISBN 0-8230-2772-4 PBK
  1. Kahn, Louis I., 1901-1974—Criticism and interpretation.
 2. Space (Architecture)—United States. 3. Architecture,
Modern—20th century—United States.   I. Kahn, Louis I.,
1901-1974. II. Title.
 NA737.K32888 1994
 720'.92—dc20   94-20094
                      CIP

Printed in Singapore

First printing, 1994

2 3 4 5 6 7 8 9 / 02 01 00 99 98 97 96 95

THIS BOOK IS DEDICATED TO
MRS. ESTHER KAHN

Woodcut created by Louis I. Kahn. Reproduction of Christmas card used by Esther and Louis Kahn in 1931.

CONTENTS

LOUIS I. KAHN AND HIS AGE

"The structure is a design in light. The vault, the dome, the arch, the column are structures related to the character of light. Natural light gives mood to space by the nuances of light in the time of the day and the seasons of the year, as it enters and modifies the space. "(1)

Louis I. Kahn was born in Estonia in 1901. When he was four years old, his parents emigrated to Philadelphia. His artistic talent made it possible for him to attend the Department of Architecture of the University of Pennsylvania. The approach to architecture at the school, then under the direction of Professor Paul P. Cret, was entirely dedicated to the tradition of the Ecole des Beaux-Arts.

"... Penn was a nice school then. It was highly religious, not as if it were a certain religion, but religious in the sense that transcendent qualities were considered worthy.... We learned to respect the works of the masters, not so much for what they did for themselves, but for what they did for others through their works, which were a high use of the language of architecture." (2)

After completing his degree, Kahn worked in a number of architectural offices, including those of the municipal architect John Molitor, and of his former professor Paul P. Cret. In 1928, Kahn returned on a trip to Estonia, his birthplace, and continued on with a tour of the Continent to England, Holland, Germany, Italy, and France. Although he had the opportunity then to visit buildings constructed under the influence of Modernism, he preferred rather to visit the famous sites of antiquity. Kahn's encounter with modern architecture took place instead on the level of publications by its adherents. He replied as follows when asked about the writings and the works of modern architecture:

"When I was first introduced to modern architecture, the books were being burned. The books that I care for a great deal somehow did not look as bright as the pages of Le Corbusier's explorations, his drawings, he speculations, his points of view. I even learned that a simple house, which was never a consideration in my training at the University of Pennsylvania, became something of importance." (3)

One may try to imagine the situation: at the same time that Le Corbusier was building the Villa Savoye, Louis I. Kahn was working in the office of Paul P. Cret, his former professor, on the design for the Folger Shakespeare Library. The disparity between these two architectural languages could not have been greater. Kahn and other architects of his generation were therefore not able to avoid the inner conflict involved in making a decision for the one or the other of these attitudes toward architecture. At any rate, construction of the Savings Fund Society Building in Phil-

Louis I. Kahn

adelphia by G. Howe and W. Lascaze marked the point at which the influence of Modernism could no longer be overlooked in Kahn's home town. And he did not remain impassive. The principles of modern architecture entered thereafter, almost of their own accord, into the world of his concepts until then so thoroughly permeated by the attitudes of the Ecole des Beaux-Arts.

"Le Corbusier was a revelation to me. He made me realize that there was a man alive who could be an inspiring teacher. Through his work he could teach you.... I felt I could throw away the books, which was what was in the air at the time Gropius advocated throwing away the books...." (4)

Even the Great Depression around 1932 was not able to delay Kahn's fundamental confrontation with the "rules of modern architecture." Together with thirty other unemployed architects and engineers, Kahn founded The Architectural Research Group (1932 - 1934).

During the following years, Kahn became involved with publicly supported housing projects and with urban design. The Rational City Plan was created during the years 1937 - 1939, as an urban vision for the accommodation of two million residents in Philadelphia. This project, at that point in time, however, did not carry the personal signature of Louis I. Kahn: rather, it represents a modified version of Le Corbusier's "Ville contemporaine" of 1922.

During 1935 to 1937, Alfred Kastner and Louis I. Kahn collaborated to plan and build the Jersey Homesteads in Roosevelt, New Jersey. This was a settlement of approximately 250 residential units, the architecture of which was entirely dedicated to the concepts of the Modern Movement. During the same period, Kahn had the first opportunity of executing a project entirely on his own: the Ahavath Israel Synagogue. The building, a pure cube in a conventional row of houses, is marked by great simplicity. The interior surprisingly radiates warmth and nobility. Since receiving his architectural degree in 1924, Louis I. Kahn did not have the opportunity to actually execute more than these two projects.
The situation changed with the outbreak of World War II. In collaboration with G. Howe and O. Stonorov, Kahn designed no fewer than seven War Housing Projects, during the years 1941 to 1942 alone. Five of them were actually constructed. Kahn finally had the chance to implement and to test certain ideas of modern architecture on a large scale.

In 1945 Kahn built an addition to the B.A. Bernard House. This addition created a somewhat awkward impression which apparently represents an important caesura in Kahn's work. Kahn did not provide skillful solutions for the problem areas treated here: the geometry of the columns, the

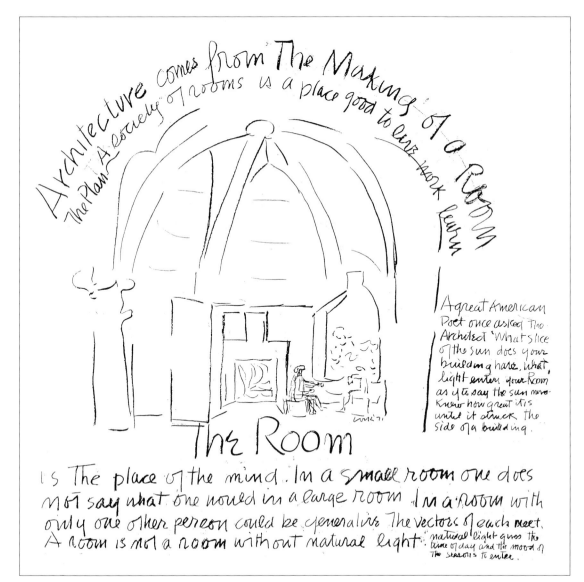

Architecture comes from The Making of a Room

The Plan A society of rooms is a place good to live work learn

A great American Poet once asked The Architect 'What slice of the sun does your building have, what light enters your Room' as if to say the sun never knew how great it is until it struck the side of a building.

The Room

is The place of the mind. In a small room one does not say what one would in a large room. In a room with only one other person could be generative. The vectors of each meet. A room is not a room without natural light. "natural light gives the time of day and the mood of the seasons to enter."

Sketch
Louis I. Kahn

strip window, the flat roof, a cube apparently hovering over a ponderous footing, the vertical clapboard siding, etc. It was only with the Weiss House (1947 - 1950) that evidence appeared which reaffirmed Kahn's architectural mastery. This success was followed by the Jewish Community Center (1948 - 1954) and by Kahn's first major work executed for the Yale University Art Gallery (1951 - 1953). By this time Kahn had indeed found his own individual and original architectural language which he would prove in the following years to develop further with extraordinary creativity.

It would hardly have been possible for an architect who had carried the attitudes and the conceptional modes of the Ecole des Beaux-Arts so deep in his own being as did Kahn, to quickly and effortlessly carry off the attempt to become an unconditional proponent of modern architecture. Indeed, with Kahn it required a very long and tedious process to integrate the modern with the tried-and-proven, and the prosaic with the noble, into a process which bore his own, individual signature.

"You can never learn anything that is not part of yourself. Everything you learn is attached, glued on, but it has no real substance in you...." (5)

Kahn began to lecture at Yale University in 1947, and eight years later he was appointed to teach at the University of Pennsylvania.

The study opportunities which Kahn enjoyed in Rome at the American Academy, as Resident Architect from 1950 to 1951, played a key role in his development. He took advantage of his foreign stay to visit Italy, Egypt, and Greece and to study the architectural legacies there. His experience with the Pyramids in Giza, the mighty columns of Karnak, the powerful pylons of Luxor, the Acropolis, and the brick vaults of the Caracalla Baths could not help but to have stimulated his thinking and feeling for the architectural world.

"Greek architecture taught me that the column is where the light is not, and the space between is where the light is. It is a matter of no-light, light, no-light, light. A column and a column brings light between them. To make a column which grows out of the wall and which makes its own rhythm of no-light, light, no-light, light: that is the marvel of the artist." (6)

Afterward, Kahn's projects increasingly demonstrated innovative and archaic characteristics, which make him more and more of a loner of his age. His search for the essence or the origin of a design problem led him on expeditions through architectural history. He gained inspiration from

My remark that structure is the giver of light is thereby recalled in the march of columns in the Greek Temple.

light no light .

no light light no light no light. in
The column is like the shine of the pen where the light is not.

Egyptian monuments, Greek temples, Roman baths, Scottish castles, fortified French cities, Gothic cathedrals, Renaissance churches, and Italian squares at a point in history when mankind prepared to enter outer space. This does not mean that Kahn's architecture simply copied the style of a particular historical epoch; rather, his efforts represented the search for the universally valid essence of a solution to an architectural problem, which he then attempted to implement through modern techniques. At the same time Louis I. Kahn fully evolved his architectural language, he also developed his own, personal form of verbal expression. He began to employ and to combine words in a new and unique manner, in order to better express his ideas and philosophical reflections. His texts are often difficult to read, to interpret, and to understand. As he stated, "Even a word is a work of art." (7)

Kahn's profound and complex manner of solving architectural problems was reflected in the methodology which he employed in his design process. His technique consisted of drawing a line with soft charcoal on sketch paper, then erasing it in the next moment in the hopes that the next line would be "the more appropriate." Kahn's complicated and time-consuming method of design, in conjunction with an intensive degree of involvement with details, had the result that he, often enough, was not able to finish a project by the agreed time. In addition, he had difficulty in accepting space assignment plans from his clients, and in working within cost limits. Many of Kahn's designs were overdimensioned from the very beginning and were much too expensive. Redrawing the plans, or even beginning again, was often unavoidable. As a result, Kahn alienated and lost many of his clients. In some cases, he continued to work on a design, although the developer had already taken the contract away from him: he simply could not part with it. There were also many projects on which Kahn worked for years on the plans without reaching a satisfactory solution. Needless to say, this working technique was not exactly economical; indeed, when Louis I. Kahn died, his office was deep in debt. He fully dedicated his life and all his efforts to architecture, and could not imagine living any other way.

Once, on returning from a project in India and Bangladesh, he went straight from the airport to his office, where he arrived at five in the morning. He found one employee still in the drafting room who had just worked through the entire night. "But where are the others?" was his astonished question.

"There is no such thing as architecture. There is the spirit architecture, but it has no presence. What does have presence is a work of architecture. At best it must be considered as an offering to architecture itself, merely because of the wonder of its beginning." (8)

If Humans are in vered

The art of building
The art of planning
The art of Business

measurable

immeasurable

varieties

einstein

प्रा

The aura
feels in a flash
The aura of the   Existence
in separable parts
its nature
Then seeks the means   preusense
to tangible reality.

Form   Design
The nature of space

The room
The society of rooms.

city   The center of availabilities
                                    meeting

Notes
Louis I. Kahn

LIGHT AND SPACE

HOW THIS BOOK CAME ABOUT

"Schools began with a man under a tree, a man who did not know he was a teacher, discussing his realizations with a few others who did not know they were students. The students reflected on the exchanges between them and on how good it was to be in the presence of this man. They wished their sons, also, to listen to such a man. Soon, the needed spaces were erected and the first schools came into existence. The establishment of schools was inevitable because they are part of the desires of man." (9)

In 1976 and 1977, during the third and fourth years of my studies at the Swiss Federal Institute of Technology in Zürich, I had the privilege to learn from the architects Ivano Gianola and Livio Vacchini, both from Tessin. They pointed out to me the work of Louis I. Kahn and helped me to become acquainted with it. For the first time, I read such poetical statements as "A building begins with light and ends with shadows," and "The sky is the roof of a square," and "A room without natural light is not a room."

Such quotations as these stuck in my mind. They left a deep impression and stimulated my interest to learn more about the man Louis I. Kahn and his work. I began to devour all the publications of his that I could get my hands on. It didn't take long to realize that I would have to see his works themselves to really understand them.

In 1980, after spending a year teaching at Syracuse University in New York, I had the opportunity of visiting and of photographing almost all the works of Louis I. Kahn in the United States. During my study trip I sketched everything of his that I saw, and step by step I began to firm up the topic which appeared most essential in these works: light in the architecture of Louis I. Kahn. His control of light, light modulation, the play of light and shadow in his buildings, the amount of light in relationship to space and structure, and the change which a building undergoes as natural light varies throughout the year.

The Esherick House (1959 – 1961) especially fascinated me: Kahn's virtuoso handling of light and space can be most impressively read in the house he designed here.

I visited the Esherick House for the first time in the summer of 1980. Even then I was sure that I would return to this house to learn and experience more about it. This home appeared full of secrets that I wanted to discover. Now, in retrospect, I know why this creation of Kahn's occupied me to such a degree: because of changing light and the progression of light throughout the year, it is a house which reveals a different side of its character upon every visit.

**Analytical sketches
U.B. 1983**

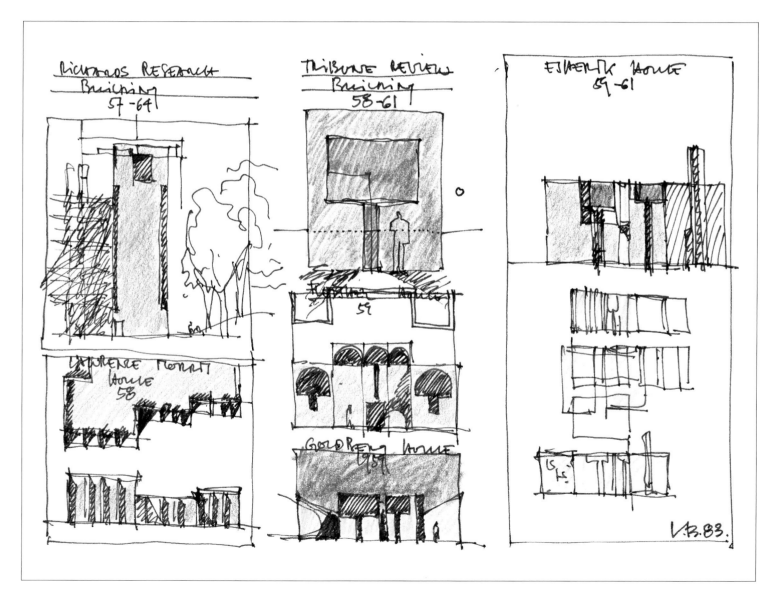

I decided to return to Philadelphia later and to use the Kahn Archives at the University of Pennsylvania to study the oeuvre of Louis I. Kahn. I wanted the time to become closer acquainted with his work through original drawings, photographs, correspondence, and information from earlier collaborators of his.

My original plan to compile comprehensive documentation only on the Esherick House, important as it was in Kahn's work, had to be abandoned quite soon, for good reason. After looking through the original sketches and microfiche evidence under the key word "Esherick House," I discovered to my great surprise that there was, initially, a planned addition to the existing Esherick House and, secondly, an atelier actually constructed for the artist Wharton Esherick. How was it possible that these two projects had remained undiscovered, until almost ten years after Kahn's death, although a book with the title *Louis I. Kahn: Complete Work 1935 – 74* had already appeared?

This discovery, more coincidental than anything else, prompted me to systematically examine all the 25,000 microfiche documents on Kahn's work. While I sat in front of the screen of the "Read and Copy Machine," I discovered a goodly number of Kahn projects which had not been previously published. By photocopying the microfiche documents, I assembled an almost complete archive of Kahn's planned and actually executed buildings. But how was I to analyze and further employ such a mass of new findings?

Finally, I decided to broaden my original idea, i.e., of investigating the Esherick House with respect to light control, design of the windows, the adjustable views from the inside outward, the integrated ventilation panels, the sunshades, and its other components. Instead, I expanded the scope of my project to cover a number of selected designs, and I soon arrived at a definition of my research topic: "Light and space in the works of Louis I. Kahn." I then felt that this clearly defined context would enable me to systematically investigate and to compare Kahn's projects.

Well-briefed by Kahn's earlier colleagues and equipped with a good map of the city, I struck out to find and examine buildings of Kahn's which had until then remained unknown. I took pictures of them and learned as much as I could about them.

During 1982 and 1983, I put together 24 files which, together with help from analytical drawings, clarified the central topic of light in the architecture of Louis I. Kahn. My photocopies of the microfiche documents served as basis for this personal study. Use of overlay techniques revealed those architectural elements which involve the topic of light. The summary texts on each of the

**Analytical sketches
U.B. 1983**

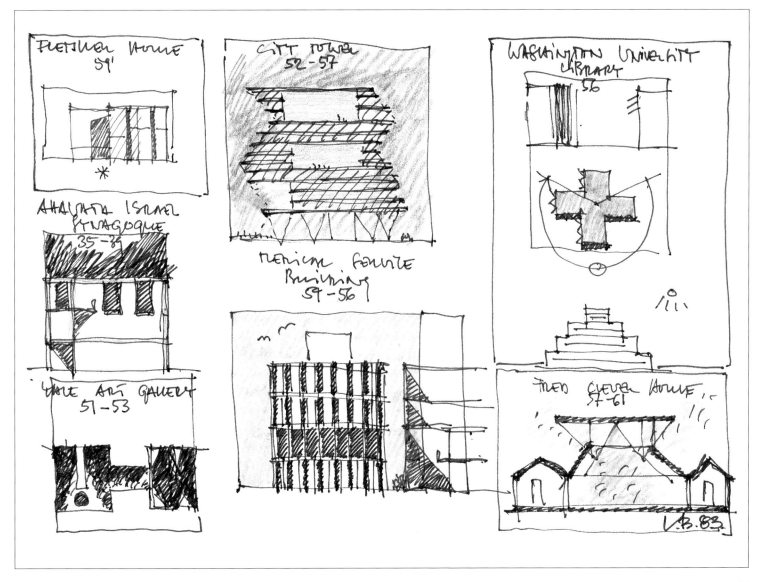

buildings investigated in this manner is my abstract, individual representation and interpretation of the insights which I gained.

In addition to drawings and collages, my work also resulted in production of a videotape with the title "One Day in the Life of a Window." With the aid of video techniques, I made exposures at the west livingroom window in the Esherick House at intervals of 30 minutes, in the attempt to record the play of light and shadows made possible by this window throughout 24 consecutive hours.

In 1985, my third Kahn-trip took me to India, Nepal, and Bangladesh. Inspecting and photographing the National Capital of Bangladesh proved to be the most difficult task of all my trips. I spent many days of my stay waiting in government offices for the necessary officials, and in explaining to them over tea and cake what I had in mind. After two weeks I finally found the right official, and I received permission to photograph in relative peace a number of the rooms of the Capitol normally off-limits to outsiders.

The Dhaka project was Kahn's most exciting and most complicated work which makes it all the more unfortunate that views of the individual, magnificent rooms of this fantastic complex have until now not been cleared for publication.

Until the moment when I was allowed for the first time to enter the Assembly Hall, I didn't even know how Kahn had solved the problem of light control above the parliament chamber (it was not possible to obtain permission to examine the construction drawings in 1983). I was therefore all the more astonished and enthused when I finally stood in this gigantic chamber, thirty meters high, and beheld how sunlight was reflected in and modulated at the same time from the exterior ring, through semicircular openings, and into the Assembly Hall.

Final material was collected for this book during my last trips to Tel Aviv in winter of 1991, and to Philadelphia in autumn of 1992.

The fifty projects I have selected from Louis I. Kahn's oeuvre for publication in this book demonstrate the extensive variety of techniques which he investigated and employed for the control and modulation of natural light. For each particular building, he attempted to find the individual coherent solution to the problems with sunlight which arose. Kahn considered the window to be an instrument amenable to fine tuning, one which could be designed to effectively provide the interface between outside and inside in ever new and changing variations.

Analytical sketches
U.B. 1983

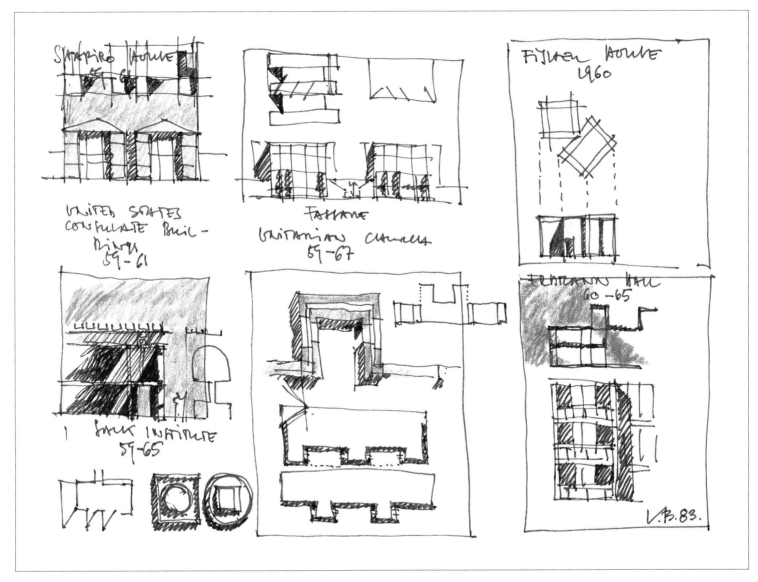

"A space can never reach its place in architecture without natural light. Artificial light is the light of night expressed in positioned chandeliers not to be compared with the unpredictable play of natural light...." (10)

The many and various methods of light control, and the different elements for light modulation, can be traced as well as mutually compared as a leitmotiv passing through Kahn's design work from beginning to end. In my analysis, I have progressed chronologically through the projects, beginning with one of Kahn's student projects from 1924, and ending with the Dhaka capitol project in 1974. My own intention throughout was to reveal and to record Kahn's untiring searches for new solutions in handling the fall of light into a room.

The window from two old words for "wind" and "eye" in its great variety of design forms represents the focal point of my study: the window as wall or ceiling opening through which light (and air) can enter the room. Louis I. Kahn spent his entire professional life in involvement with this element of illumination and ventilation. He considered the individual window to be a formal and functional entity, one which, in turn, became a highly essential component of his spatial structure.

"A plan of a building should be read like a harmony of spaces in light. Even a space intended to be dark should have just enough light from some mysterious opening to tell us how dark it really is. Each space must be defined by its structure and the character of its natural light." (11)

In his early work, Kahn resorted to solutions, more or less conventional, which took the form of separate, protruding sunshade elements. In his later projects, however, he invented and developed a number of integral sunshading measures which have endowed his architecture with its unique and intensely personal character. Kahn's many different experiments also included the functional and formal integration or separation of window and ventilation openings.

Archaic openings and forms particularly characterize the architectural impression made by those of Kahn's buildings which were subjected to extreme climatic conditions, and for which sunlight must be filtered such as his work for Angola, India, Pakistan, Bangladesh, and Israel. Giant "light filters" were designed here which on the one hand furnish shadow and, on the other, ensure sufficient ventilation and a view toward the outside.

**Analytical sketches
U.B. 1983**

"The order of light was respected in the buildings I did in India and Pakistan, now Bangladesh, by giving the outside building to the sun and the interior building to habitation." (12)

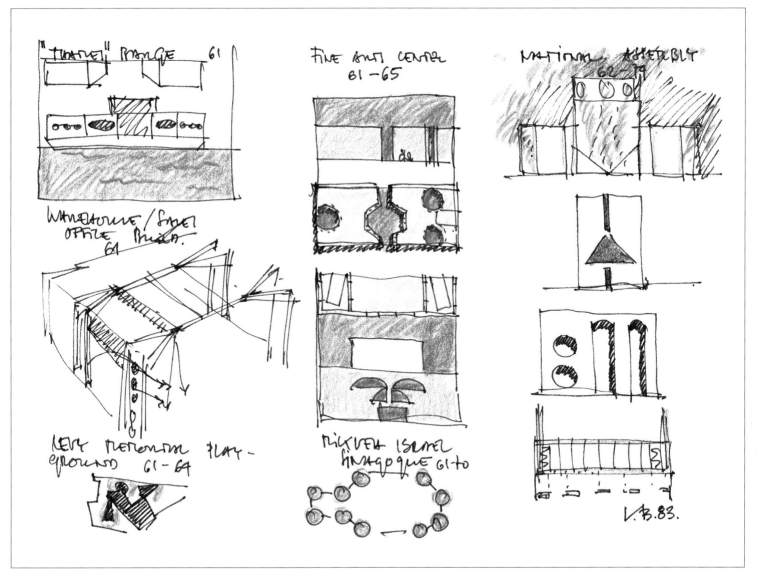

"THEATE" RANGE 61

FINE ARTS CENTER 61-65

NATIONAL ASSEMBLY 62-74

WAREHOUSE / SALES OFFICE BLDG. 61

LEVY MEMORIAL PLAY-GROUND 61-64

MIKVEH ISRAEL SYNAGOGUE 61-70

V.B.83.

25

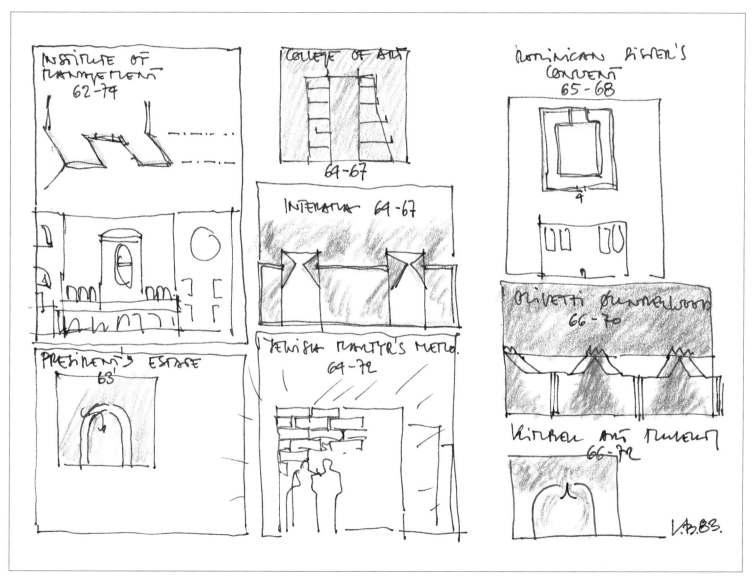

INSTITUTE OF MANAGEMENT 62-74

COLLEGE OF ART 64-67

DOMINICAN SISTER'S CONVENT 65-68

INTERAMA 69-67

PRESIDENT'S ESTATE 63'

JEWISH MARTYR'S MEMO. 69-72

OLIVETTI HEADQUARTERS 66-70

KIMBELL ART MUSEUM 66-72

LAB.83.

TEMPEL BETH-EL ST.
66-74

EXETER LIBRARY
67-72

HUROS SYNAGOGUE
68-74

WOLFSON CENTER
68-74

CENTER FOR
BRITISH ART
69-74

DUAL MOVIE THEATER?
70

FAMILY PLANNING CENTER
70-74

56
~60

Die Schädige-
Traum
1924-36

V.B.83.

27

In the late work of Louis I. Kahn, it becomes apparent that skylight plays an increasingly important role, and that Kahn develops ever more sophisticated solutions for light control and modulation. The culmination of all Kahn's experiments is without doubt the Assembly Hall in Dhaka. Here, we quite vividly see how Kahn incorporated the experience gained from his earlier designing and building, in the creation of a genuine architectural jewel.

This book was organized in accordance with the sequence of my own steps of work. The sketches at its beginning (and those for the Esherick House) are intended to show nothing other than an approach, through drawing, to those buildings which I analyzed, a process of approach from which my theme of light originated and gradually developed.

The layout of this book as published reflects the content of the 24 files which were assembled in 1982 and 1983. The documents (plans and sketches) are presented on the left page of the book, and my personal interpretations are found on the opposite page: at the top right, a small emblem as abstraction of the theme "light and space." Page 29 explains the analytical technique with original plan, overlay plan, photograph, as well as emblem with the symbols employed.

For the projects which followed the Esherick House, more space was allotted to the photographs, and detailed drawing analyses were no longer provided.

The end of the book contains a typology of the various light control and modulation elements employed by Kahn.

"Material lives by light," wrote Louis I. Kahn. "You're spent light, the mountains are spent light, the trees are spent light, the atmosphere is spent light. All material is spent light." (13)

Analytical technique
Original plan by Louis I. Kahn
Analytical plan
Emblem
Photo
Symbols

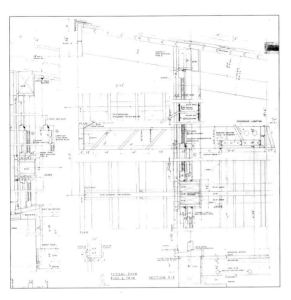

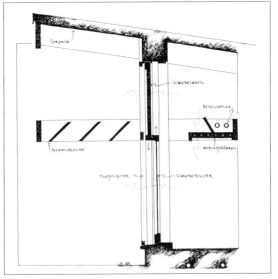

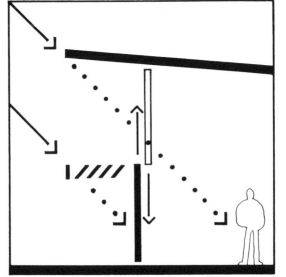

Curtain

Northern light

Direct light

Broken light

Movable panels

Movable panels

Leaf for ventilation

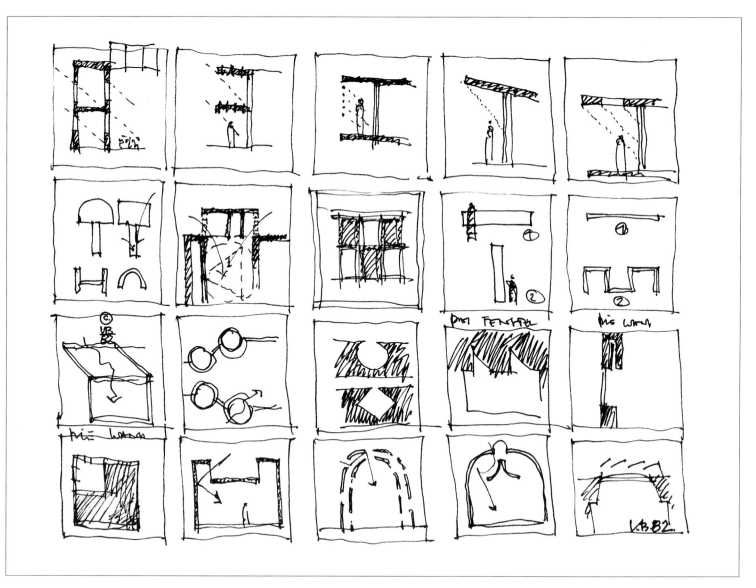

Projects

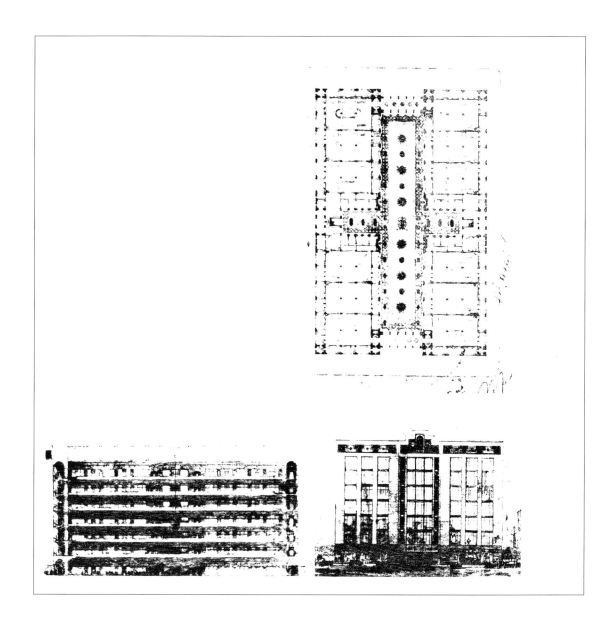

To the best of my knowledge, this is one of the only two projects known from Louis I. Kahn's student work under Professor Paul P. Cret. It is entirely in the spirit of the Ecole des Beaux-Arts. The facade is designed according to the three-fold classical breakdown into base, main order, and attic. Kahn's project features austere axial-symmetrical configuration, with no particular orientation to geographical directions. On the ground floor, Kahn integrates a portico which appears in all four facades. An interior-court gallery extends through all seven floors and is perhaps intended to be covered by a barrel-vaulted glass roof. The gallery divides the building into two shop and office blocks, which are bridged over the two main entrances. The stairways, elevators, and auxiliary rooms are configured as servicing elements in the middle of the two oblong building units. Arcade corridors provide access to office rooms. It appears that the windows in the two office blocks are intended to extend from the floors to the ceilings. Shading elements for protection against direct sunlight are not apparent, a lack which allows the pilasters prominence in their monumental verticality. It is only in the area of the access bridges that modulation of light is possible, by virtue of the double walls (see drawing on the right page).

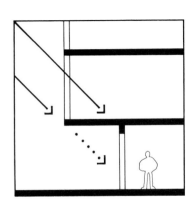

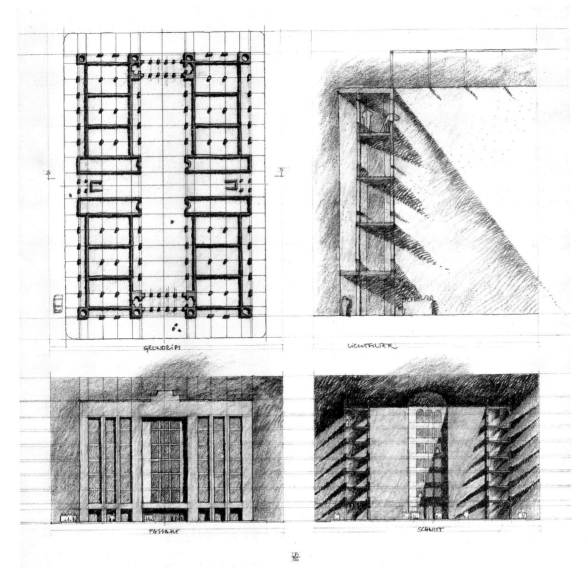

GRUNDRISS

LICHTFILTER

FASSADE

SCHNITT

Plan
Section
Elevation
Analytical drawing

JERSEY HOMESTEADS
1935 – 37; BUILT
ROOSEVELT BOROUGH,
NEW JERSEY
WITH A. KASTNER

The development Jersey Homesteads became the new home for many Jewish families who emigrated from Europe. This cooperative essentially consisted of about 200 homes, a school (also serving as community center), a modern plant for production of clothing, and a farm.

The bungalow-type homes were built in park-like landscape, adjacent to a circular village street, and were quite spacious for their time. Most were one-story, and none had basements. The walls consisted of concrete blocks, and the non-isolated flat roof is a slightly protruding concrete slab. The construction technology as well as the architectural language represents Kahn's first attempt (in an actual context) to implement the principles of modern architecture on a large scale, to test their effects, and to gain experience in their use. The outward form of each home is the result of the configuration of rooms inside, which have been clearly broken down into daytime and nighttime areas. The long garage appears to have been added on at the side of the floor plan. The windows of the dining and living room extend from the floor to the ceiling. Some window parts are non-opening, and some have casements. Kahn installed no sunshades here to protect the large glass surfaces from direct sun. The other windows appear to have been stamped out of the walls. A small lintel spans the window opening.

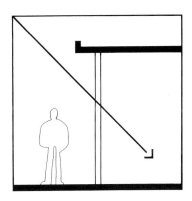

Plan
Housing units
Window detail

AHAVATH ISRAEL
SYNAGOGUE
1935 – 37; BUILT
PHILADELPHIA,
PENNSYLVANIA

**Entrance facade
Interior**

It was as a 34-year-old architect, that Louis I. Kahn was first able to build on his own. (At the same time he also collaborated with Alfred Kastner on the Jersey Homesteads in Roosevelt, New Jersey.) The plans for this early design, an attempt to implement concepts of modernism in a synagogue, are no longer extant. This synagogue, a pure cuboid with a flat roof, stands in a conventional line of row buildings. The brick entrance facade is designed as a massive face wall. Three small windows provide light for the stairwell. The south longitudinal facade, also brick, is completely closed. The north facade, however, is plastered and calls an industrial structure to mind, with its visible supports and non-loadbearing infilling walls. The north facade contains windows which furnish light for the foyer, the synagogue chamber on the first upper floor, and the gallery above. The windows extend to the ceiling, creating "ceiling-framed" windows, an economical solution since the ceiling also provides the lintel. The interior radiates surprising warmth and a distinguished atmosphere: inside, the industrial character of the north facade appears forgotten. Wood paneling integrated into the structural configuration features precisely placed spotlights and ventilation openings in interplay with the massive north windows, and bathes the room in warm light. The wall on the courtyard side of the room, where the Bima (lectern) is located, is provided with glass brick.

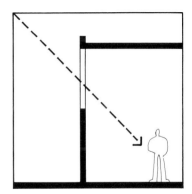

PREFABRICATED HOUSE
STUDIES
1937 – 38; UNBUILT
WITH L. MAGAZINER
AND H. KLUMB

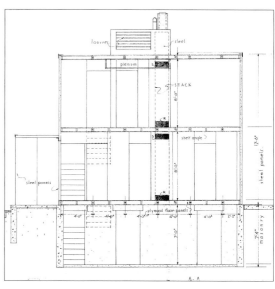

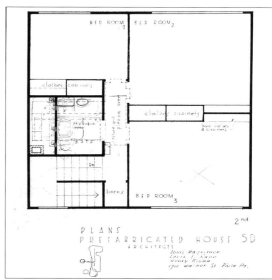

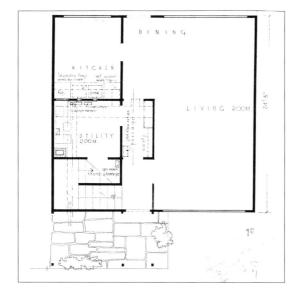

This study project was supported by S. Fels, who had voiced his interest in an economical mode of construction. By now, thirteen years had passed since Louis I. Kahn had received his diploma. Why this long interruption? For one reason, Kahn had worked for a relatively long time in various architects' offices; for another, this was the Great Depression, during which construction was at low ebb.

Kahn's "Prefabricated House", an assignment which he posed to himself and a number of his colleagues, was the result of his own thinking on social issues. Here we see the first attempts to integrate objectives of modern architecture into mass-produced housing. The typical row house is provided with a flat roof and extra-large windows, in order to meet expectations for light, space, and air. On the ground floor, the windows are over-proportioned and are fully exposed to light (and cold), perhaps the reason why curtains are shown in the plans. The traditional porch is employed (but without any embellishment). For the first time, the otherwise customary double-hung (sash) windows were replaced by strip windows with vertical muntins. The bathroom, in the interior, receives light through a conventional but overdimensioned skylight. My schematic drawing attempts to show the disproportional ratio of the window openings to the total wall area.

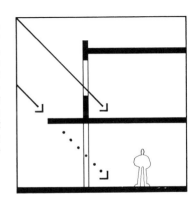

Elevation
Section
Ground floor
Top floor
Analytical drawing

J. OSER HOUSE
1940 – 42; BUILT
ELKINS PARK,
PENNSYLVANIA

Kahn's first single-family house is characterized by exceptional architectural variety. Structural and formal unity as in Ahavath Israel Synagogue appears discarded here in favor of experiment. Kahn combined rough-stone masonry work with timber construction for this flat-roofed house, for which he employed a great variety of window types and forms. The northeast facade is characterized by a timber-constructed cube protruding beyond the house footing, and by two window strips, one above the other, which wrap around the corners. Here, for the first time, Kahn negates the "old" rule of loads and supports in order to evoke effects of lightness and weightlessness through "new" approaches characteristic of Modernism. The horizontal window extend-ing over the entire facade section reinforces this intention (Type C: see analytical drawings to the right). On the ground floor (southwest), the huge corner window wraps around the living room like conservatory glazing. The concept of "flowing space" between inside and out appears here for the first time (Type D). The windows, recessed into the rough-stone masonry wall, are located and dimensioned according to the functional conditions of the interior rooms, and are not interrelated. On the ground floor, they give the appearance of being punched out of the masonry (Type B). On the upper floor, they extend to the ceiling (Type A: "ceiling-framed" windows). The emblem shows the corner window (Type D).

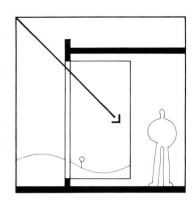

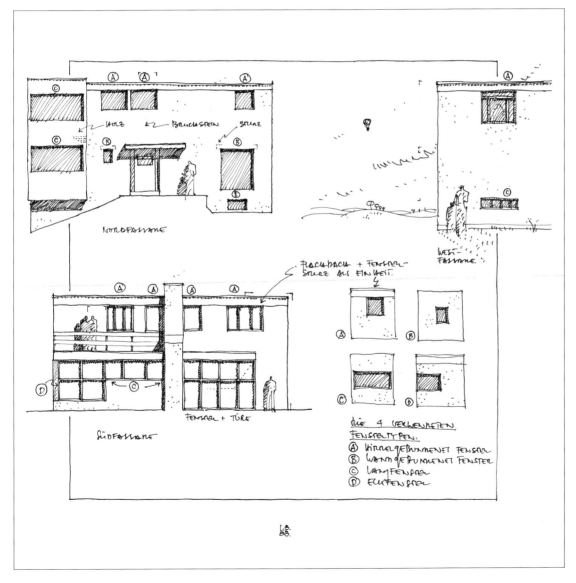

Ground floor
Top floor
Exteriors
Analytical drawing

L. BROUDO HOUSE
1941 – 42 ; UNBUILT
ELKINS PARK,
PENNSYLVANIA

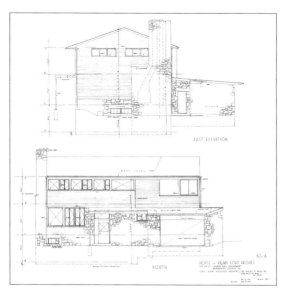

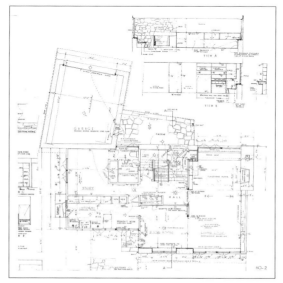

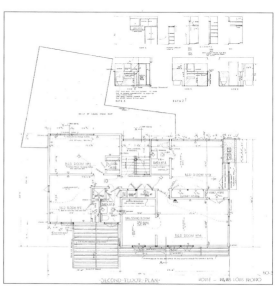

The Broudo House was intended to be built very near the Oser House. The Broudo House, designed a year later, appeared conventional in comparison. A timber house with horizontal siding, gable roof, and a garage situated at the front at somewhat of an angle (owing to the geometry of the property and the orientation of the house to the south). Upon closer examination, however, one finds an element with which Louis I. Kahn will be involved for years: the brisesoleil, configured here horizontally. The south facade, provided with a strip window (ratio of window area to masonry area approx. 2 : 1), is protected by one of these elements. Here as well, the windows extend all the way to the ceiling. The brisesoleil is a simple timber structure with cantilevered brackets and rebated boards set at angles. In front of the kitchen, the brisesoleil of the dining and living space is extended to form a type of pergola roof (see plan of upper floor), and provides shade for an outside seating area. In order to shade the window areas on the upper floor (two windows in square form, and one strip window), the gable roof projects asymmetrically toward the south. The projecting roof covering here appears too small to provide sunshade function, especially for the large square window at the left in the south facade. Kahn will continue to involve himself in ongoing experiments with the topic of a roof projecting over a strip window.

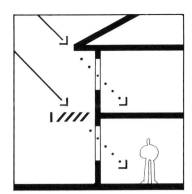

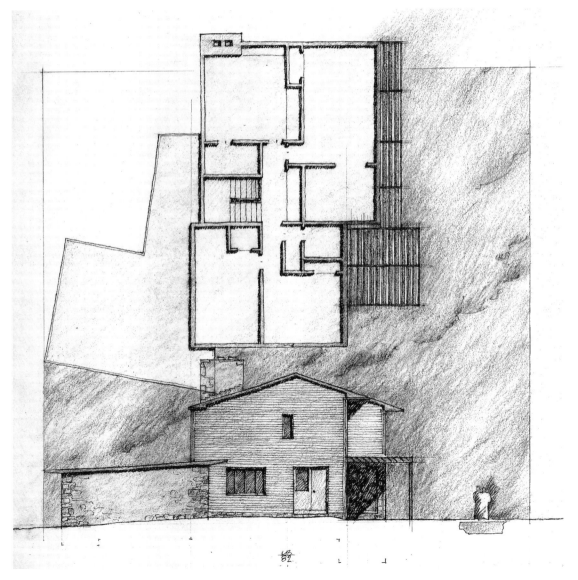

Elevations
Ground floor
Top floor
Analytical drawing

CARVER COURT
HOUSING
DEVELOPMENT
1941 – 43; BUILT
CALN TOWNSHIP,
PENNSYLVANIA
WITH G. HOWE AND
O. STONOROV

This development, located near a medical center for wounded veterans, originally served to accommodate the medical staff. Carver Court is only one of several of Kahn's developments very quickly executed during World War II. Kahn therefore had the opportunity to continue searching for his own architectural language. Of all the merely planned or actually executed war housing projects (Pine Ford Acres, Stanton Road, Lily Ponds, Pennypack Woods, Berry Farms, Willow Run, Bomber City, and Lincoln Highway Defense Housing) Carver Court is one of the most interesting.

Only two house types can be treated here. The free-standing four-family house is intriguing due to its stark, cubic appearance. The main facade is interrupted on the ground floor only by one strip window (cf. original plan) which, however, was eventually replaced by two small square windows.

The row house stands on overly massive masonry cross walls, which accommodate only garage, entrance area, and furnace room. The living and bedroom areas lie above. The verticality of the footing section contrasts with the window strip installed in the horizontal clapboard siding. The window strip consists of a series of conventional double-hung (sash) windows installed next to each other. The slightly protruding roof serves no convincing formal or functional purpose: it is ineffective as brisesoleil and, as fascia, the extending roof makes too weak an effect.

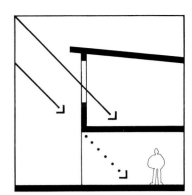

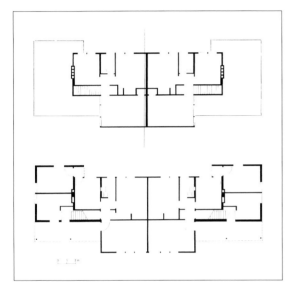

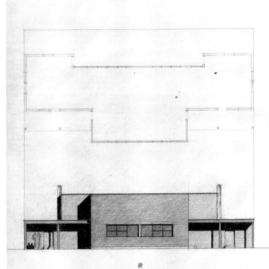

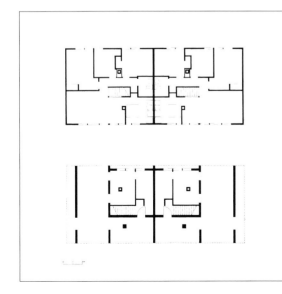

South elevation (Type A)
South elevation (Type C)
Plans (ground and top floors)
Analytical drawings

HOTEL FOR 194X
1942 – 43; UNBUILT
WITH O. STONOROV

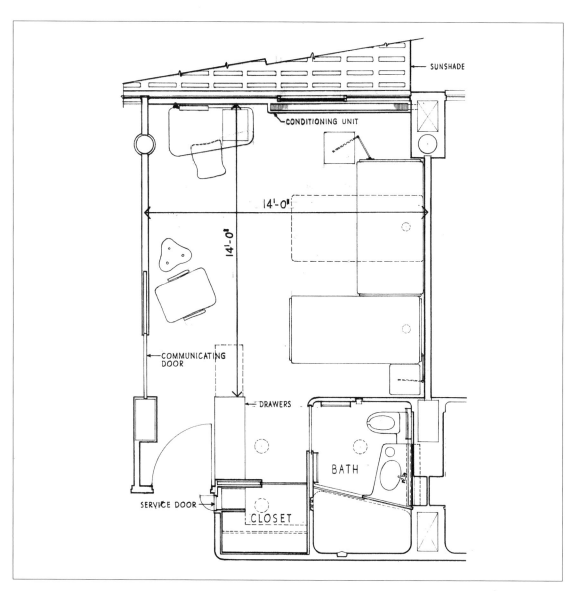

SUNSHADE

CONDITIONING UNIT

14'-0"

14'-0"

COMMUNICATING DOOR

DRAWERS

BATH

SERVICE DOOR

CLOSET

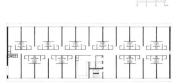

In 1942, Kahn and Stonorov were invited by the journal *Architectural Forum* to submit a design dealing with the topic of prefabrication. Although the two architects were not originally able to meet the deadline for publication, they found the opportunity one year later to complete the project and submit it to the same magazine. They submitted a design for a typical hotel of the 1940's: hence the name "Hotel for 194X."

The public spaces are accommodated in the ground floor, which is dominated by the thirteen-story block installed above. The floor plan of the floors is conventionally designed: the guest rooms are lined up in an east-west direction along the corridor. The concrete floor slabs, supported by columns, are designed as brackets tapering toward the outside. As a result, the space in each room becomes higher and brighter toward the facade. In addition, this construction allows use of strip windows, which extend over the entire length of the cube. Brisesoleils are installed in front of the windows to diminish the effects of direct sunlight. This formally strong, horizontal element consists of corrugated aluminum sheeting perforated by small rectangular slots. These cut-out openings create a geometric play of lights and shadows on the facade, according to the height of the sun, which point to similar effects in the Radbill Therapy Building built five years later.

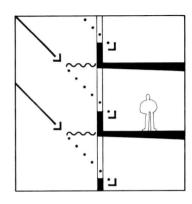

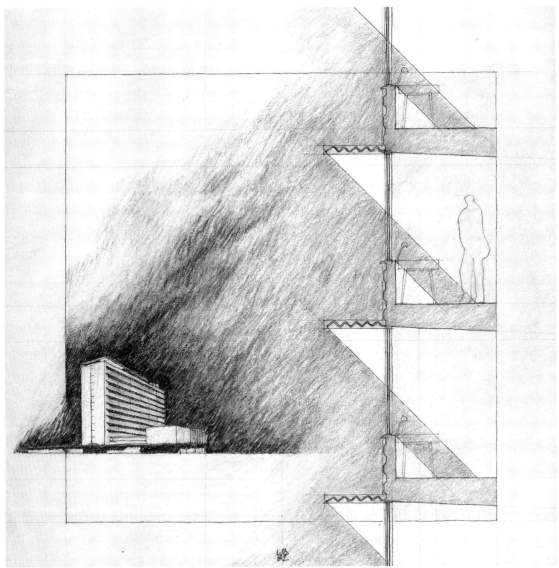

Typical plan
Plan of a room
Analytical drawing

INTERNATIONAL LADIES
GARMENT WORKERS
UNION HEALTH CENTER
1943-45; UNBUILT
PHILADELPHIA,
PENNSYLVANIA
WITH O. STONOROV

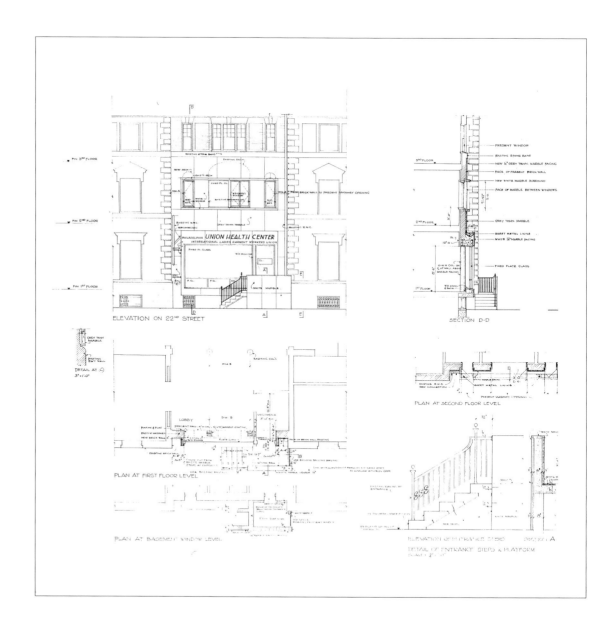

Detail of elevation
Section
Plan
Analytical drawing
West facade

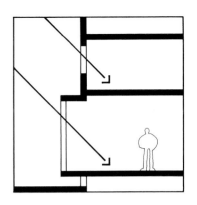

The task here was to redesign the entrance to the Union building, the first time that Kahn was confronted with an existing building and, at that, a brick building designed according to classical rules. Kahn planned to completely redesign the symmetrical entrance of the classicistic building. He employs a huge steel lintel in installation of a large show window, with a door shifted out of the symmetry axis. A white marble frame surrounds the window and door, and projects boxlike from the facade. (The stairs and facing of the landing parallel to the building frontage line anticipate the entrance Kahn later designed for the Yale Art Gallery.) Although the modifications to the windows on the first upper floor result in no structural-engineering changes, the vertical window configuration gives way to the horizontal. Another marble frame, also protruding from the facade, emphasizes the singularity of the new "false" strip window. Kahn consciously attempts to confront the traditional brick building with concepts of modern architecture, based on utterly different materials consciousness. Conflict becomes evident between different concepts and languages of architecture.

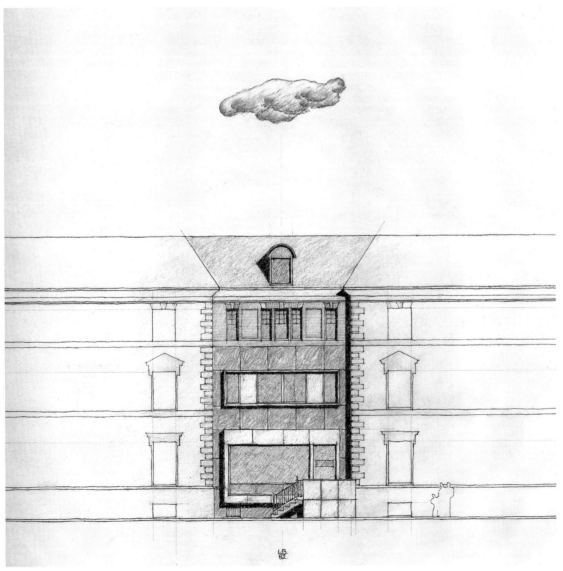

PARASOL HOUSES
1944; UNBUILT
WITH O. STONOROV

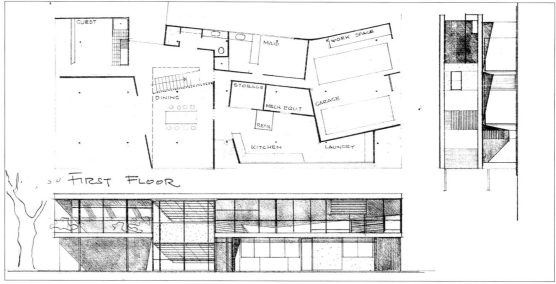

FIRST FLOOR

As shown by various of Kahn's designs from the early forties, he attempts here to incorporate programmatic aspects of Modernism into his architectural language. Again, his designs are the result of fictitious assignments free from the expectations of an actual developer which allows him to experiment with new architectural concepts. It appears that ideals of the Beaux-Arts tradition have now been left far behind. The design shown here is based on Le Corbusier's fund of ideas and calls to mind the Domino House of 1916 and the Citrohan House of 1922. Non-loadbearing, strangely angled walls are inserted into a grid of concrete columns. Kahn utterly lacks Le Corbusier's talent for employing elegantly curved walls as contrast to the rigid arrangement of building supports. The two-level living and dining room with gallery, the stairway at an angle into the room, and the one isolated column in the middle of the living room all create an awkward effect. Two brisesoleil elements seriously disturb the intended verticality of the window which extends over two stories (planned to contrast with the horizontal ceiling and the roof).

The setback of the walls behind the ceiling and roof edge creates a play of shadows which takes into account the concept of the projecting concrete slabs. At the age of 43, Kahn stands once again at the beginning of adventure into the new and unknown.

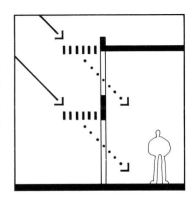

Perspective
Plan
Elevations
Analytical drawing

PHILADELPHIA
PSYCHIATRIC HOSPITAL
1944 – 46; UNBUILT
WITH O. STONOROV

Axonometric projection
West facade

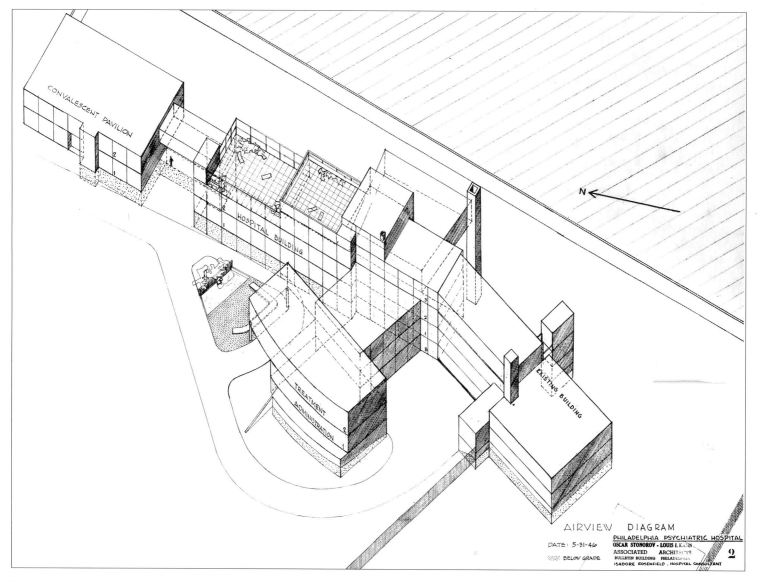

AIRVIEW DIAGRAM

PHILADELPHIA PSYCHIATRIC HOSPITAL
DATE: 5-31-46   OSCAR STONOROV · LOUIS I. KAHN
ASSOCIATED ARCHITECTS
BULLETIN BUILDING PHILADELPHIA
BELOW GRADE   ISADORE ROSENFIELD · HOSPITAL CONSULTANT

2

This extension, if executed, would have connected into the north side of the existing hospital. Kahn planned a covered automobile accessway, a foyer with reception, offices for physicians, treatment rooms, ward rooms, and day rooms for the patients. The peculiar angularity to the geometry is the result of the shape of the property. The double-storied therapy room is situated above the entrance area, the staff rooms, and the doctors' offices. A salient feature of this therapy room is the sweeping wall, toward the west, which is without openings up to eye level. The windows installed at a slant under the roof create a shadow which provides a distinct termination to the facade for this section of the building. The projection in this case is surely not intended for purposes of sunshade: instead, the primary motivation here is the concept of threefold subdivision (base, main order, and attic). Projecting sunshade elements are installed in the patients' wards (northwest facade), over the strip windows. The sunshades appear excessively narrow in relation to the height of the window area.

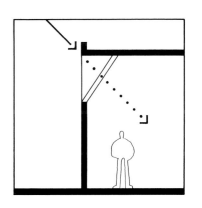

B.A. BERNARD HOUSE
1945; ADDITION
KIMBERTON,
PENNSYLVANIA
WITH O. STONOROV

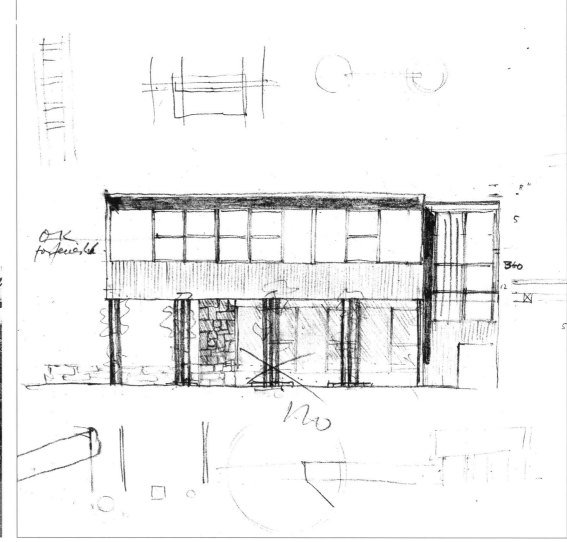

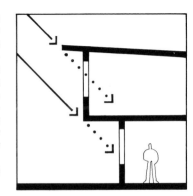

In my opinion, the Bernard House represents one of the most peculiar designs produced by Louis I. Kahn.

The Bernard project entailed an addition to an existing house, the original plans for which were no longer extant. The footing to the house consists of rough stone, which supports a wooden structure protruding beyond the footing on all three free sides. The arrangement of the columns is particularly curious: for example, at positions at which the overhang is greatest, there are only two columns; where the projection is less, there are five. In addition, the columns increase in diameter toward the top, in order to carry the loads by half-over and half-under support. The odd number of columns must have displeased Kahn, since he crossed through the middle one with the comment "No" written on the plans. The upper floor brings to mind the row houses in Carver Court. The distinctive aspect of the south facade is the strip window which extends its entire length. The muntins also represent a peculiar feature: they take no account of the columns below. Moreover, the rooms with different depths all have the same window size. The overhang of the almost-flat roof could be considered a brisesoleil. Unlike the Carver Court project, the clapboard siding is vertically instead of horizontally installed: an aspect which was at that time intensely debated among Modernists in the USA.

Subsequent alterations have radically changed the addition.

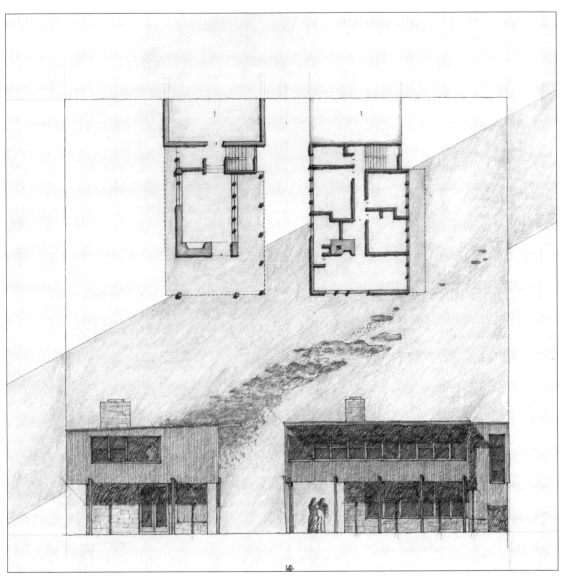

South view
South elevation (late version)
Analytical drawing

PENNSYLVANIA
SOLAR HOUSE
1945 – 47; UNBUILT
WITH O. STONOROV

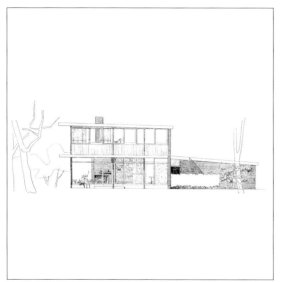

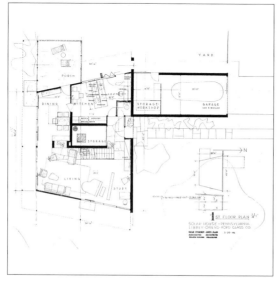

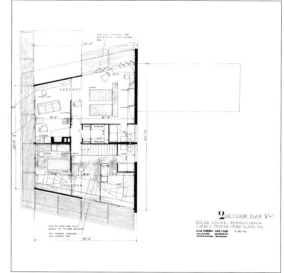

In 1946, the Libbey Owens Ford Glass Company sponsored a study to investigate the feasibility of thermopane glass as it involves building materials technology, lighting engineering, and particularly architectural implementation. The company invited 49 architects to submit designs. The Pennsylvania Solar House project included new, future-oriented, as well as already-known elements. The most noteworthy characteristic is the thick brick wall facing the north, with its small bathroom windows, and the openings in the entrance area. The east and west facades are conically oriented toward the sun; as does the south side, they feature continuous glass fronts. In order to shade these huge window surfaces from direct sunlight, Kahn provided four kinds of control elements: the projecting brisesoleil with obliquely installed slats over the ground floor (cf. the Broudo House), the flat roof with projection far out beyond all sides of the upper floor (cf. Carver Court), as well as two new developments by Kahn. These were the sliding folding wall in front of the west window, and the horizontally sliding wooden panels located at the interior of the windows (ground floor and east and south facade). Although folding shutters do not reappear in any of Kahn's later designs, the sliding panels do show up in modified, further-developed form in other of his designs as guiding concepts.

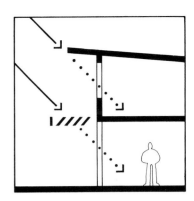

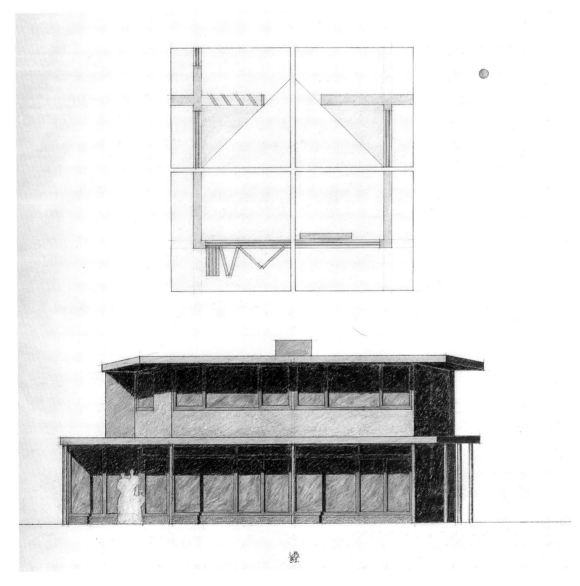

East elevation
North elevation
Ground floor
Top floor
Analytical drawing

Q. ROCHE HOUSE
1947 – 49; BUILT
CONSHOHOKEN,
PENNSYLVANIA
WITH O. STONOROV

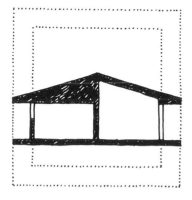

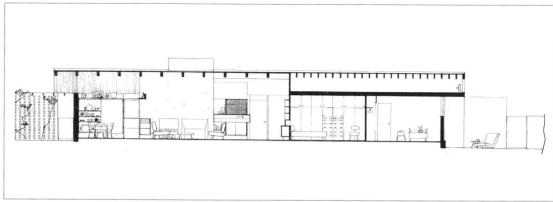

At first glance, one would not expect this single-family dwelling to have been designed by Louis I. Kahn and yet this project marks an important milestone in the architect's search along his way between Ecole des Beaux-Arts and modern architecture.

In the Roche House, the wall experiences a new interpretation as a filter between inside and out, in the form of a single-layer glass membrane with a maximum of transparency. Under a symmetrical gable roof, the cross walls and windows are installed partly on an outer and partly on an inner boundary line, with emplacement of the roof between these walls as reinforcement of the intended architectural concept. Here, Kahn experiments with five different types of openings to admit light into interior space including a skylight over the entrance area. Noteworthy is also the huge fireplace, displaced from the main geometry of the house. In addition to the natural light of the day (the sun), natural light in the night (fire) is a topic which occupied Kahn all his life. Fire as primeval element, with all its physical and psychological connotations, never ceased to fascinate Louis I. Kahn.

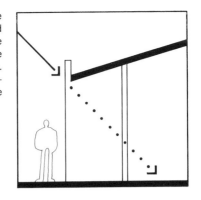

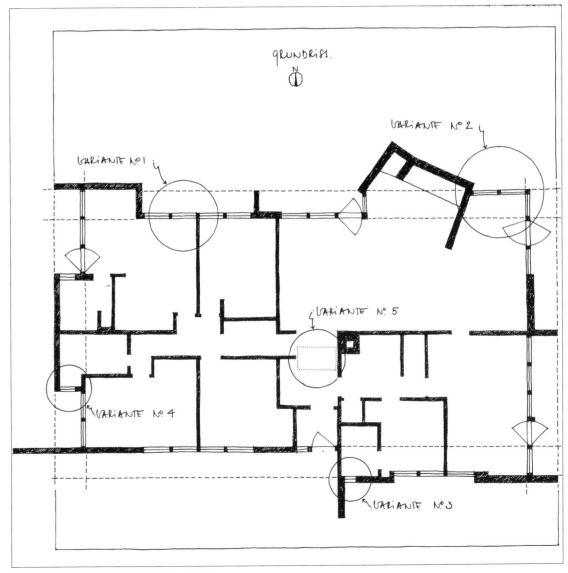

grundriss.

N

VARIANTE N° 1

VARIANTE N° 2

VARIANTE N° 5

VARIANTE N° 4

VARIANTE N° 3

East-west section
North view
Analytical drawing

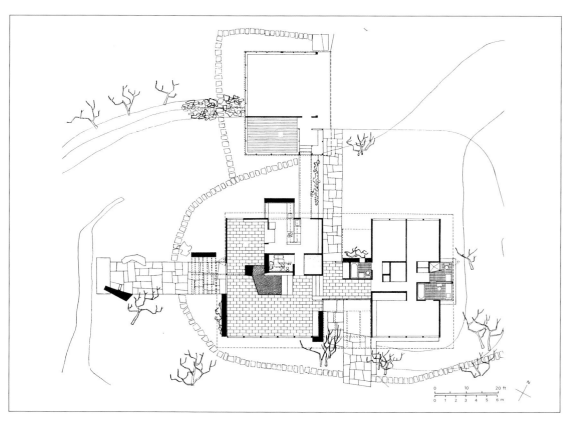

The Weiss House is perhaps the most interesting project as well as the last from Louis I. Kahn's early work. Beginning with the Jewish Community Center of 1948 - 1954 and the Yale University Art Gallery of 1951 - 1953, Kahn's work, without obvious transition, moves into its late phase.

The Weiss project is packed full of ideas and insights stored up from the previous 24 years. Involvement with Modernism appears to have been resolved. The floor plan is functionally divided into three wings: garage, living/dining area, and bedrooms. The rough-masonry walls remind us of early designs by Mies van der Rohe with cross walls which reach up out of the landscape like wings. The core of the house is a mighty, sunken fireplace. For the first time, Kahn makes a design and drawing for a wall painting as integral part of the interior. The cutout in the roof on the south side, between the living room and the bedrooms as well as the pergola beam spanned on the west side call to mind the work of Frank Lloyd Wright. The V-shaped roof appears almost identical to that of the Maison Errazuris designed by Le Corbusier in 1930. This V form allows light to penetrate as far as the longitudinal axis of the house. The primary design concepts, however, are realized in the large, two-story living room. For the first time, Kahn's brisesoleils appear with transversal wooden louvers. A low-temperature heating system, cast in concrete, serves as counterweight for the extreme overhang. Indi-

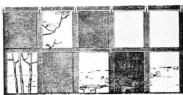

Plan
South facade
Living room
Explanatory drawing

**Section
Detail drawing
Analytical drawing
South facade detail**

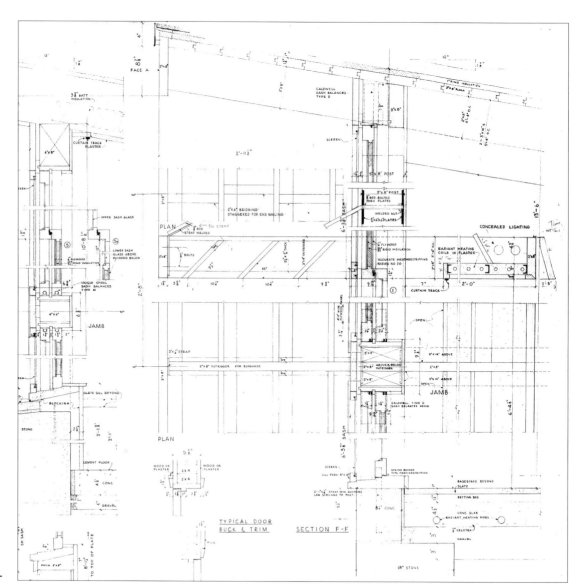

0 1 2 3m

rect lighting is integrated above. A far-projecting canopy protects the facade from sunlight and weather. The roof rafters are visible throughout the interior as visible structural elements; together with the facade supports, they form a spatial grid. A high eaves fascia provides a pronounced horizontal border to the roof. More important and more interesting, however, are the vertically sliding wooden panels in the windows. Kahn elaborates on his concept here in three drawings. The window area at the outside right is glazed over two stories. As the occupant desires, the panels may be shifted to optically connect or divide the interior from the exterior. There is a total of 14 variations for arranging the interior in its relationship to landscape and sky. The interior facade

therefore becomes a huge picture frame in which picture sections can be selected and combined at will. Extreme variations: entirely open during the day, and closed completely for protection at night. The technical expenditure for this wonderful idea, however, is enormous (see detailed plan). It did not take long, in fact, until the wood warped, and the mechanism no longer functioned. Kahn, nevertheless, implemented this concept in two later projects.

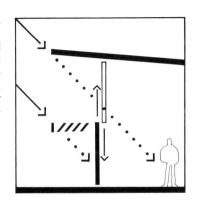

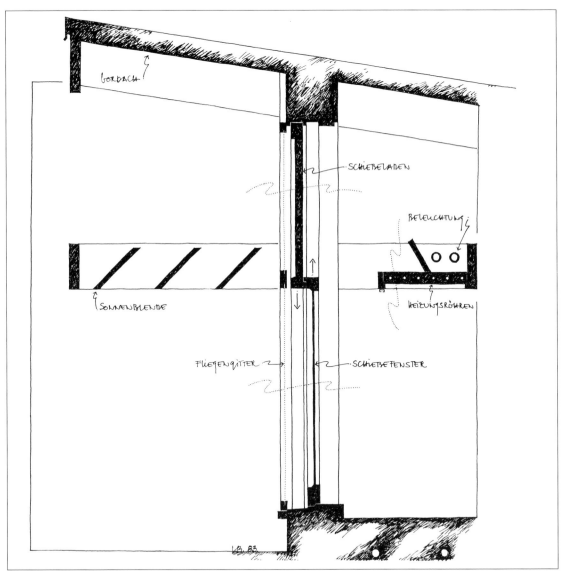

S. PINCUS BUILDING,
PHILADELPHIA
PSYCHIATRIC HOSPITAL
1948 – 54; BUILT
PHILADELPHIA,
PENNSYLVANIA

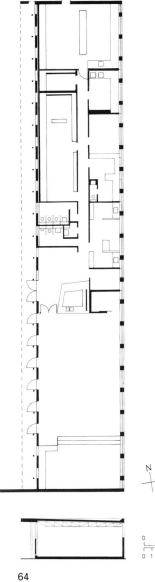

This oblong building is spanned by trussed girders which appear structurally to rest on the window frames. These girders, however, actually transfer their loads through the canopy roof to freestanding steel columns. The Pincus Building is a further attempt by Kahn to realize the concept of sliding window sections, with modification here in the form of simpler technical implementation. The lower row of windows is provided with large-leaf, door-type panels which have either of two positions: open or closed; sliding is not possible (the window installed above is non-opening). The wooden panels and frames outside the non-opening door and window structures, however, can be moved back and forth in relation to each other, by means of a pulley and cable control system.

"A room which can quickly assume a different aspect for different functions is a psychological asset, because it satisfies a natural craving for variety. With shutters up and doors open, the recreation area merges with the outdoor terrace. With the shutters down and the doors closed, patients see a paneled wall that gives a sense of security at night." (14) Three basic patterns therefore result: during the day (with closed doors), a chessboard pattern. With opened doors, a continuous and transparent pattern. And at night (with the wooden panels lowered), a medium-height wall.

Plan
Section
West facade
Interior
Analytical drawing

S. RADBILL BUILDING
PHILADELPHIA
PSYCHIATRIC HOSPITAL
1948 – 54; BUILT,
ALTERED
PHILADELPHIA,
PENNSYLVANIA

Detail of brisesoleil
Section
Plan (1st upper story)
Northeast facade

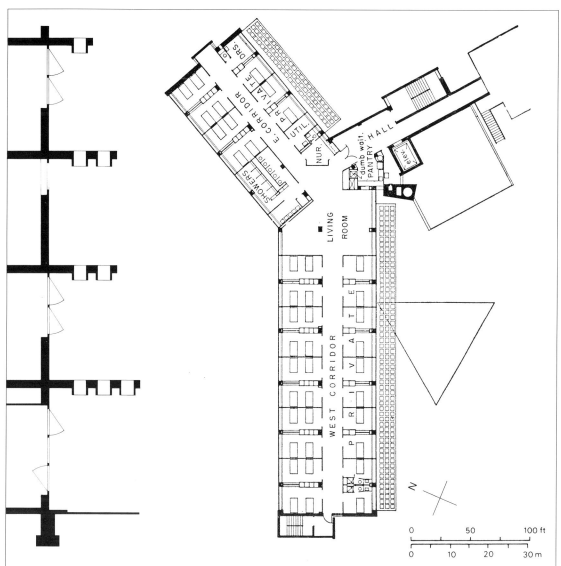

The preliminary design prepared four years earlier is replaced here by a functionally superior Y solution. Moreover, Kahn now attempts, in this second hospital addition, to unite the original Pincus Building with its first addition to form a unified ensemble of three parts. The design is based on a concrete-skeleton construction with a row of columns arranged along the central axis. The strip windows, extending entirely to the ceiling, are installed above slate-paneled apron walls. Ventilation is provided by pivoting open the top-hung windows from the bottom outward. To protect the strip windows from direct sunlight, the concrete floor slabs project beyond the plane of the facades on the east and west sides. In his preliminary design, Kahn had already included the concept of brisesoleils; the eventual solution, however, was formally and constructively more interesting. The projecting concrete slabs support suspended hollow wooden cubes. These "light filters" are dimensioned such that, at particular times of day, only a fraction of the incident sunlight will fall onto the facade. The result is a wonderful geometric light pattern formed on the dark background (slate and glass). A conceptional inconsistency are the brisesoleils which taper toward the top, although the strip windows have the same height throughout all floors. The windows of the south-west facade are not sunshaded.

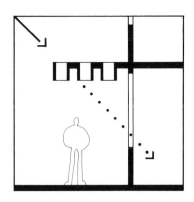

YALE UNIVERSITY ART
GALLERY
1951 – 53; BUILT
NEW HAVEN,
CONNECTICUT

The Yale University Art Gallery is Louis I. Kahn's first major contract outside his home town of Philadelphia. Clarity and power distinguish Kahn's Yale design. Owing to required flexibility in the space assignment plan, Kahn designed units consisting of two large rooms each. These units are divided by a cylindrical stairwell and a central service block ("serving spaces and served spaces"). In response to the existing neo-Gothic facade, Kahn executed a great brick wall structured only by four horizontally installed water-drip molds. The facade of the entrance section is set back in order to highlight the transition between old and new. The north and east facades are entirely glazed. The difference between, "closed" and "open" could not be more pronounced. The mighty masonry wall as element for definition of street space, as well as complete glazing of the facade: these represent radically new developments in the architectural language of Louis I. Kahn.

The large windows originally provided at Yale proved to be problematic owing to the sacrifice of wall space and the difficulty of light regulation. As a result, they are for the most part now covered by panels.

Access to the rooms is via a freestanding, intrinsically enclosed, round stair tower. Kahn designed the stair spiral as an inscribed triangle. The structure of the tetrahedron-shaped roof construction is given thematic treatment by Kahn here. A ring of glass bricks forms the end of the cylinder and allows natural light to enter. The con-

Southwest elevation (sketch, late version) Northeast facade

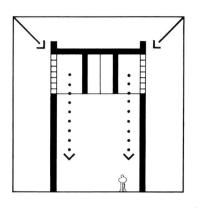

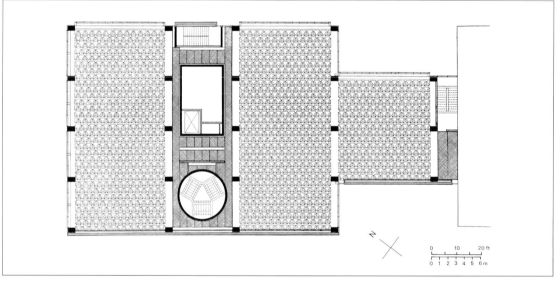

Typical plan
Stairway
Top closure of stairway cylinder

crete plates of the triangular construction serve as "light blades" which deflect the light downward. The interior space of the triangle lies in shadow; the cylinder and the triangular form sharply contrast.

The tetrahedral concrete ceiling slab has continuous hollow spaces in the longitudinal direction which accommodate ventilation ducts and spotlights. The resulting three-dimensionally modulated ceiling structure represents a stark contrast to the wall and window sections, which remain plane. The ceiling edge is executed as an underprop in order to implement as delicately as possible the elements of the glass envelope and its muntins. Hanging textile strips are provided as sunshades between the last tetrahedral joist (canted toward the inside) and the window extending from the floor up to the lower edge of the projection. These strips can be adjusted by rotating and sliding. Kahn proposed this sunshade element here for the first and last time: it proved ineffective. Wide white curtains were installed in their place.

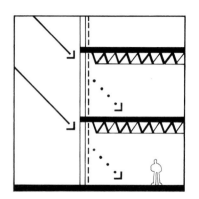

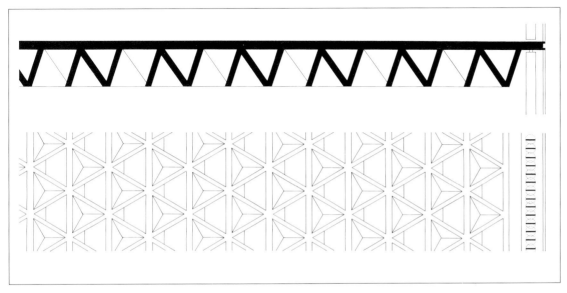

Floor construction
Northwest facade
Window detail

L. FRUCHTER HOUSE
1951 – 54; UNBUILT
PHILADELPHIA,
PENNSYLVANIA

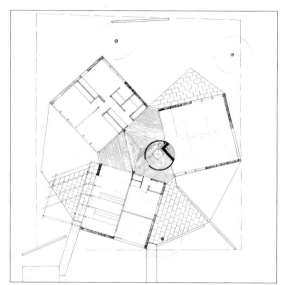
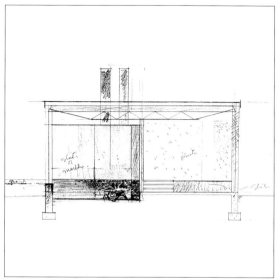

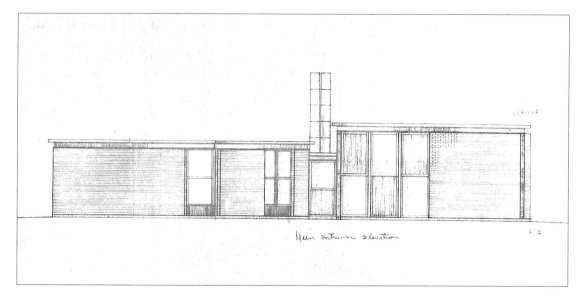

Main Entrance Elevation

In my opinion, the Fruchter House represents an exceptionally interesting design: for the first time, Kahn has designed a project with definitely clear geometric figures, one which features a center providing radial access to peripheral rooms. The star-shaped floor plan is composed of the basic forms circle, triangle, and square, and it is arranged according to the functions of the particular rooms. The triangular interior room serves as entrance area and access to the remaining rooms. The two-story living area, on a slightly lower level, is accommodated in the first wing of the house. The second wing contains the kitchen, dining room, and guest rooms. The bedrooms are in the third. The cylinder-shaped furnace room with its part of the fireplace (oriented to the living room) has been located away from the central area of the house. The Fruchter House is Kahn's last design which attempts to implement the concept of vertically sliding wooden panels. Contrary to the Weiss House and the Pincus Building, there are no sunshade elements at all in the Fruchter House. The sliding shutters and the windows have been incorporated flush into the facade, in order to emphasize the clarity of the cubic construction. It is curious that Kahn proposed to structurally span the large dimensions of the living room with the aid of a wooden construction featuring a cable under tension. The location of the garage at the edge of the property is highly practical.

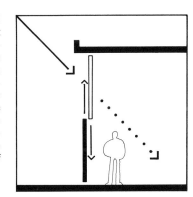

Plan
Section
Northeast elevation
Analytical drawing

AMERICAN FEDERATION
OF LABOR
MEDICAL SERVICES
BUILDING
1954 – 57; BUILT,
DEMOLISHED 1973
PHILADELPHIA,
PENNSYLVANIA

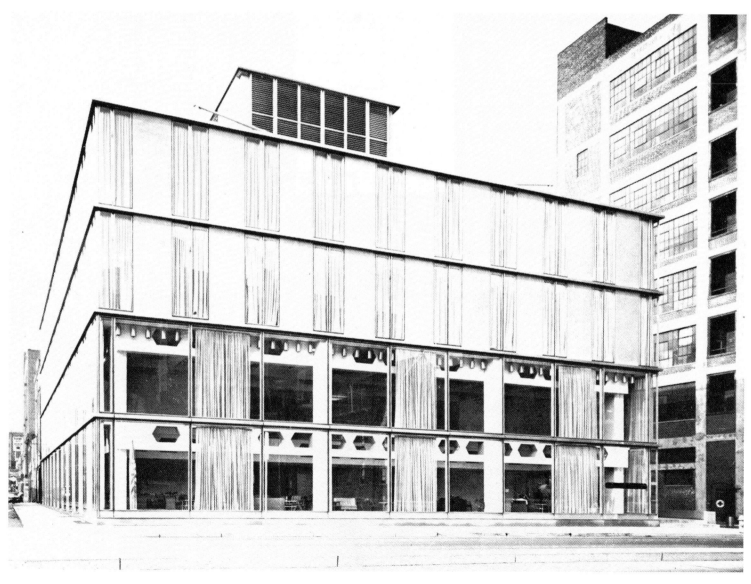

The flexibility required in the interior space of this building prompted a design from Louis I. Kahn similar to the Yale University Art Gallery. The ventilation ducts are accommodated in the recesses of the Vierendeel joists. In this design, the concrete floor slabs appear in the form of thin underprops in the facade. Cross walls and glass are alternately installed in narrow strips. This design may appear at first glance to represent a clear concept; in reality, however, it presented many and various conceptional problems which were never satisfactorily solved here. At the east and west facades, the Vierendeel beams run flush behind the vertically extended window and wall sections. Instead of revealing the total strength of the intermediate floor-slab construction in the facade, or of solving the conflict between the construction height of the Vierendeel joists (plus floor-slab thickness) and the facade skin in front, e.g., by providing additional projection of the floor-slab edge Kahn halfheartedly moved the Vierendeel beams one column width back in the north facade. The joist itself is "stuck" to the left and right of the columns. In addition, these beams in the two-story foyer have no structural function and were provided strictly for decoration. Sunshade and privacy are provided only in the form of curtains. Kahn solved the problems outlined above only later exceptionally, to be sure, in the Yale Center for British Arts and Studies.

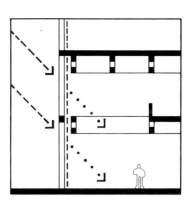

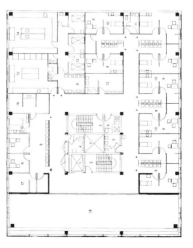

North facade
Foyer
First upper story

N

JEWISH COMMUNITY
CENTER
1954 – 59; BATH HOUSE
AND DAY CAMP BUILT
EWING TOWNSHIP,
TRENTON, NEW JERSEY

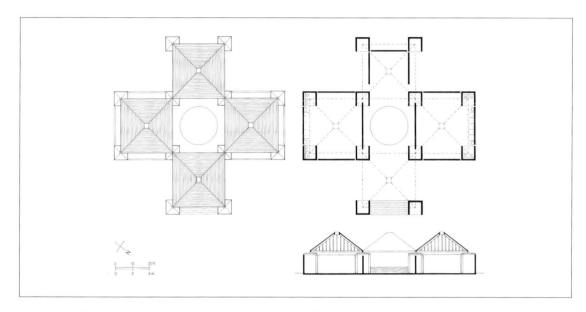

Top view of roof; plan; section
Southwest view
Analytical drawing
Stairway

Of the entire originally planned community center complex, only the bath house, pool, and Day Camp were actually built. Kahn's design for the bath house is distinguished by its central symmetry. The interior courtyard is surrounded by four structures covered by pyramid-shaped roofs: one room for ticket sales, two changing rooms, and the open stairway entrance. Twelve massive hollow columns support the roofs. For the first time, Kahn designs a skylight as an integral part of a structure but not entirely successfully, as we shall see. Duality with walls becomes a central matter here, as we know them from Kahn's design for the Roche House. For the ticket-sales building, the walls are "inside"; in the changing rooms, they are "outside" on three sides. The roof edges run in all cases along the central axis of the powerful pillars. This displacement of the walls to the outside is not without difficulty. For one, it confuses the concept of the central skylights, due to light entering from the side. For another, it exposes the sanitary fittings to the elements. Control of light is successful here only in the ticket-sales building and in the covered stairway exit where the walls stand inside the edges of the pyramidal roof, or were left out altogether. Nevertheless, Kahn writes: "After the completion of the Trenton Bath House, I never had to look to another architect for inspiration." (15)

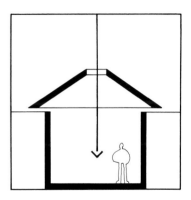

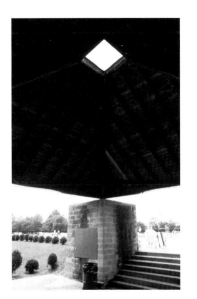

L. MORRIS HOUSE
1955 – 58; UNBUILT
MT. KISCO, NEW YORK

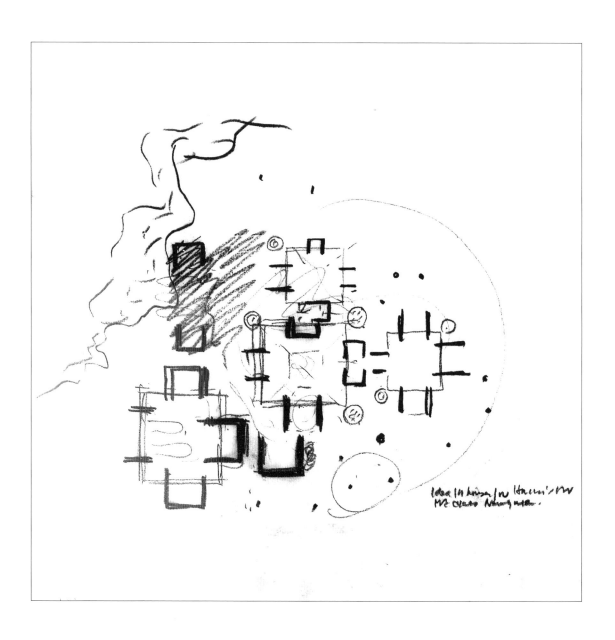

The severe geometry and formal discipline which Kahn exhibited in the Yale University Art Gallery, in the Fruchter House, and in the Trenton Bath House appear to have dissipated here. With the exception of the bedroom section on the west side, the floor plan and the silhouettes of the facades are characterized by an apparent lack of order. The massive vertical walls evoke images of a medieval castle on the peak of a mountain. Upon examination of the model from above, however, the intention becomes apparent of according each room its own identity through variation of room height. The architectural concept of the Norris House is based on the employment of cross walls which, arranged next to each other as they are here, leave open vertical light slots which stand as piers at right angles to the glass facade. The freestanding bundle of cross walls in the east section of the project should be interpreted to only a limited degree as serving for sunshade: primarily, it represents an element which by virtue of its dramatic verticality amalgamates and emphasizes the concepts of interior and exterior. The window niches here, still open to the top at this stage of Kahn's work, form the basis for further development. In this context, compare with the First Unitarian Church and School in Rochester, for which the wall and the window have become double-layered.

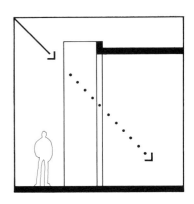

Sketch (late version)
Plan
Top view of model
Southwest facade of model

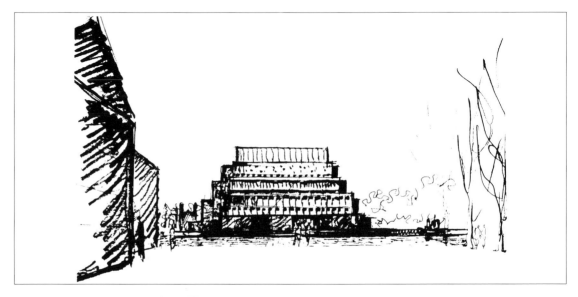

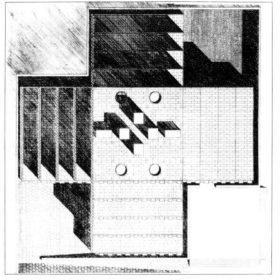

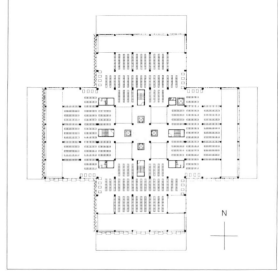

Louis I. Kahn's design for the Washington University Library was submitted as part of a competition. In order to integrate the new construction into the existing facilities, Kahn provided it with a stepped exterior, reminiscent of a ziggurat. The pattern resulting from the cut-out corners lends the floor plan a cruciform. In order to allow light to penetrate sufficiently into the relatively deep building, a double-story room directly behind the facade is provided after every second story. Kahn, furthermore, did not design the middle area of the centrally symmetric construction to permit light to enter from above into the interior of the building. To shade the windows from direct sunlight, Kahn proposed brisesoleil panels, slightly staggered with respect to each other, for installation on the south side. For the west facade, Kahn planned a vertically configured light filter consisting of V-shaped metal elements. Strangely, however, he designed no elements to shade the east facade. Kahn continued to employ the ziggurat form and, unlike at St. Louis, he treated the possibility of a light source from above in later projects: see the project descriptions on the Common Library for Graduate Theological Union (GTU), as well as on Phillips Exeter Library.

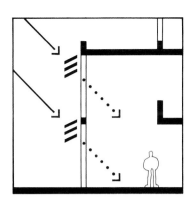

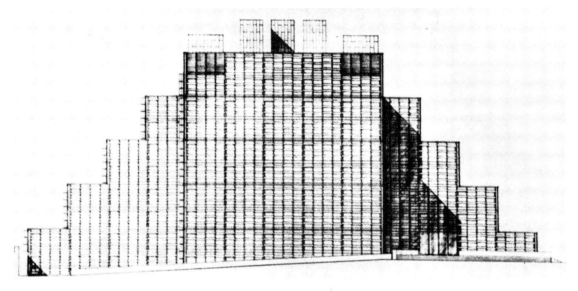

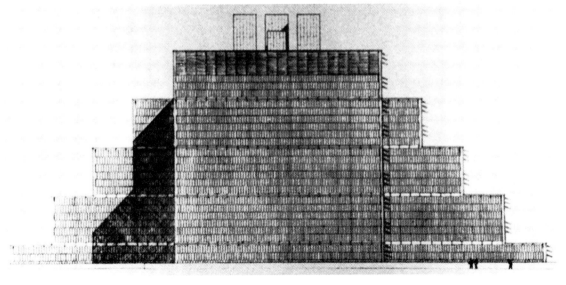

South elevation sketch (late version)
Top view of roof; plan
South elevation
West elevation

C. CLEVER HOUSE
1957 – 62; BUILT
CHERRY HILL,
NEW JERSEY

Plan
Section
South facade
Living room

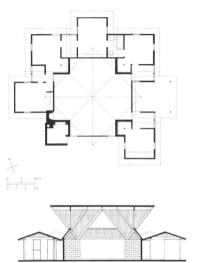

After they had seen the Bath House in Trenton, the Clever family commissioned Louis I. Kahn to design their own home. The geometrical discipline of this earlier project is moderated for the Clever House. Here, Kahn grouped "satellites" around the centrally symmetric living room: these are structures dimensioned according to their respective functions, and designed with pyramidal roofs. The living room is characterized by surprising spaciousness, in contrast to the surrounding annex constructions, which make a somewhat impractical impression. The cruciform-designed roof of the living room rests on four massive L-shaped concrete leaves of blocks. The ridge purlins, which protrude far out of the room, protect the triangular windows from direct sun-light and from the elements. The documents here depict the structural features of the roof construction, based as it is on the geometric form of the triangle. At the side of each non-opening triangular window in the living room, Kahn installed wooden panels which can be opened to provide sufficient ventilation for this high space. Kahn pursued this idea further in later projects: see the material on the Esherick House and the Fisher House. Although these windows cannot be opened, their design executed for the first time here allows them to merge with the integrated ventilation panels to form a functional and formal unity.

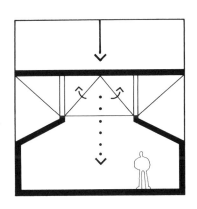

A. NEWTON RICHARDS
MEDICAL RESEARCH
BUILDING AND BIOLOGY
BUILDING
1957 – 65; BUILT
PHILADELPHIA,
PENNSYLVANIA

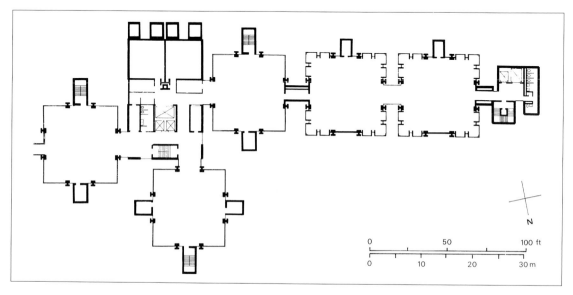

This design is characterized by structural clarity. The working space of the institutes is organized on the basis of the square, and can be flexibly subdivided as required. This space is flanked by imposing brick towers containing supply and exhaust ventilation ducts and the emergency staircase. The functional effectiveness of the laboratory rooms, however, has proved to be a highly problematic matter. At any rate, the architectonic impression rendered by these towers calls to mind the sketches of towers made by Louis I. Kahn in San Gimignano on his first trip to Europe, in 1928. A concrete skeleton construction has been integrated into the brick towers, which ponderously weigh on the earth. The concrete skeleton, however, by virtue of Vierendeel supports tapering toward the periphery, evoke a sense of horizontal lightness. The brick parapets have been installed flush with the windows onto concrete brackets. The interplay between the interior room structure and the exterior envelope is demonstrated expressively here. On the other hand, the windows are not protected from the sun: the special blue-tinted window glass proved to be insufficient. The occupants were later forced to install aluminum foil on the inside of the windows. To achieve maximum transparency and lightness, the sheets of window glass at the top were directly connected at the corners with silicon sealing compound and L-formed metal clamps, instead of framing.

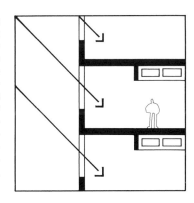

Plan
Concrete skeleton
Laboratories
Window detail

TRIBUNE REVIEW
PUBLISHING COMPANY
BUILDING
1958 – 62; BUILT
GREENSBURG,
PENNSYLVANIA

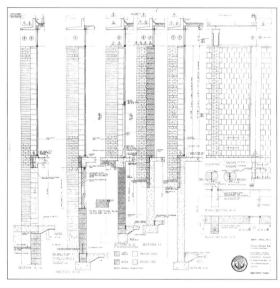

As in the Trenton Bath House, Kahn uses rough concrete blocks here. Prefabricated, prestressed concrete beams bridge the long span from the exterior walls to the service core. These beams rest on supports which are built up of relatively small masonry blocks, and which appear in the exterior facade as projecting structural elements. The non-loadbearing walls are installed into this structural system. These walls feature the first appearance of a window type which is a true invention of Louis I. Kahn: the keyhole window. The loophole windows of the Morris House are amalgamated with the strip windows of Modernism to produce a new entity. The ponderous verticality of the Ecole des Beaux-Arts is apparently united with the horizontal lightness of modern architecture. Perhaps Roman architecture also served as an inspiration to Kahn. His keyhole windows allow an eyelevel field of vision toward the outside, they permit sufficient wall area to profitably furnish the floor space, and the window area above the furnishing ensures optimal illumination of the room. Kahn's earlier experiments with sliding wooden panels, and his use of windows extending directly to the ceiling, may have contributed to development of this window type. From this point on, Kahn further developed and refined his keyhole window, in various modifications and in a great variety of projects. At the Tribune Review Building, skylights are also installed above the service block.

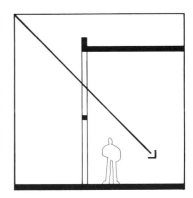

Ground floor
Detail drawing
Northeast facade
Interior

H. FLEISHER HOUSE
1959; UNBUILT
ELKINS PARK,
PENNSYLVANIA

A Ledge for roof plank (not for
   the garden units)
B Reglet for roofing
C Fixed window or brick panel
D Operating window slot

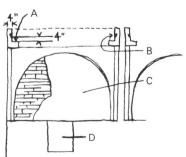

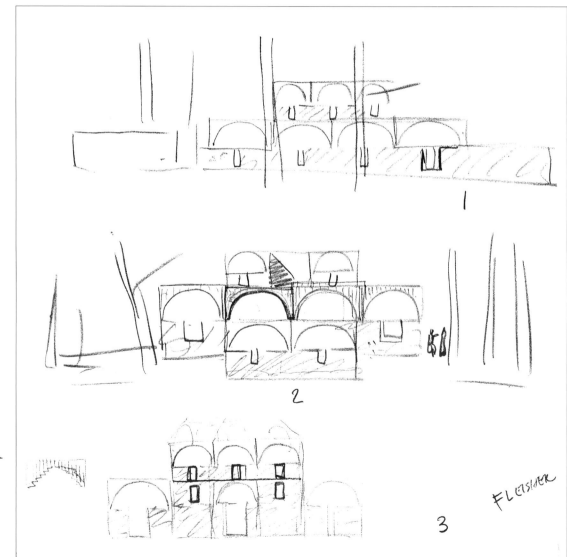

The axially symmetric design of the Fleisher House is strict. In order to emphasize the central axis, Kahn planned for exaggerated separation of the two squares on the basis of which the living room lower by a half story is conceived. It is not apparent from the outside, however, that this is a split-level home. The keyhole window first employed for the Tribune Review Publishing Company Building appears here as well, but in further-developed form. The semicircles call to mind Roman brick structures. The footing consists of masonry, and the concrete cross walls above the footing feature semicircular cutouts. Brick walls or non-opening windows could be installed into these cross walls. Kahn does not indicate how such non-opening windows might be shielded from the sun. The window slots below serve for an outward view and for ventilation. Kahn varies the form of this opening in the footing area according to functional requirements. In Kahn's gazebos, the semicircles as well as the viewing slots have been left open; or, he extends them to the floor to serve as doors. Above the entrance, they combine to admit sunlight and to allow looking out. Kahn's recourse to the three basic geometrical forms (square, circle, and triangle) opens the way toward developing a new architectural language: one which will become more and more powerful. His efforts of many years to fall in with Modernism now appear to have finally ceased.

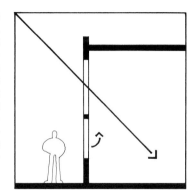

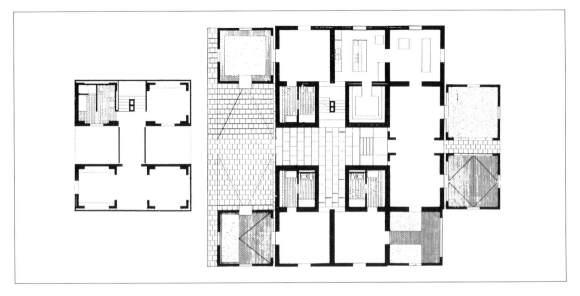

Explanatory sketch
Sketch (late version)
Ground floor and upper floor
Model

Of all Kahn projects, it was the Esherick House which most extensively occupied me during my studies of his work. Two primary characteristics distinguish this house. First are the novel window systems with their various possibilities of linking or separating "outside" and "inside" by means of adjustable ventilation panels. Second is the distinct separation between "serving spaces and served spaces" in the floor plans and sections.

In 1982 I began to chronologically arrange the original Esherick sketches still existent at the Kahn Archives in Philadelphia. Even the earliest contained the keyhole windows and the four layers (for "serving spaces and served spaces"). Kahn clearly classified structural elements as loadbearing or non-loadbearing here. As with the Tribune Review Building, the columns on which the concrete joists rest are composed of concrete blocks, in turn assembled from small parts. The non-loadbearing walls are inserted there, and feature viewing and ventilation slots in the middle. Non-opening windows are installed above. During the design process, Kahn gradually transformed a skeleton structure into a conventional masonry construction: a development clearly apparent between the analytical sketches no. 9 and no. 14. The two-story living room, in addition, is shifted from the north toward the south. Kahn logically integrates the stairway into the middle, "serving" zone (analytical sketch no. 15). The large masonry-wall and window sections clearly organize the respective east, south, and

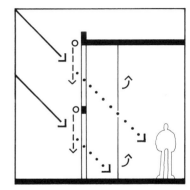

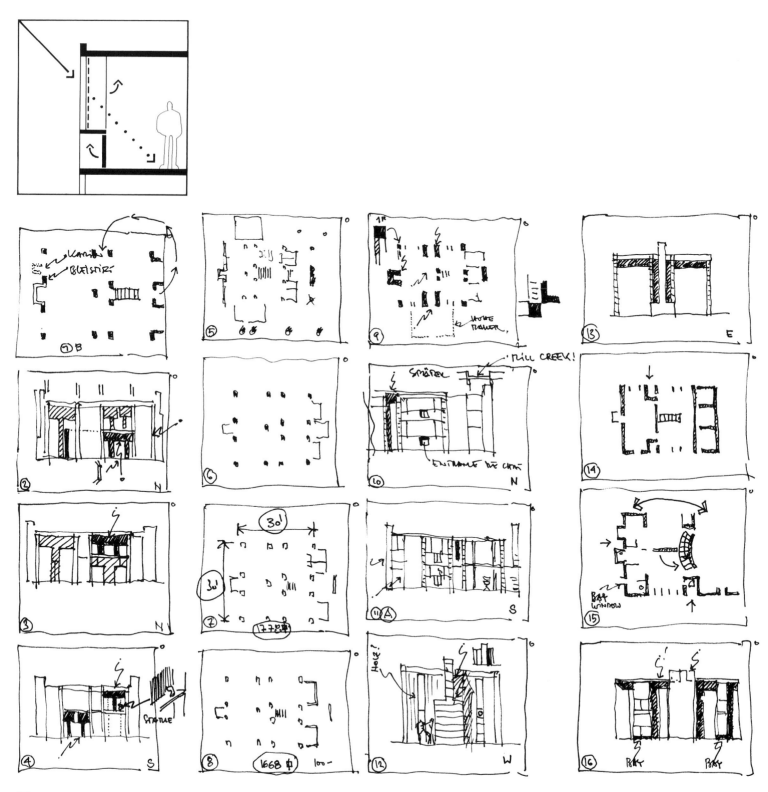

west facades. The north facade, however, is minimally provided with doors and conventional windows located according to interior functional requirements.

For M. Esherick, Kahn also further developed the detail of wooden ventilation panels next to non-opening windows (cf. the Clever House for the original employment). All glazed surfaces (except on the north facade) are non-opening. Rolling fabric shades are provided for sunshade on the outside of the southeast facade. Non-glazed ventilation shutters, next to the windows in vertical niches, allow cross-ventilation. The ventilation panels can be opened and closed horizontally to enable extensive variation in control of the occupant's visual contact with the surroundings of the house. This concept permits marvelous visual experience in conjunction with the keyhole window in the two-story living room. Kahn designed the west interior facade as an entity consisting of windows, bookcases, and ventilation opening. Once the two ventilation panels, located one above the other, are closed, the occupant has no visual connection with the outside: the interior makes an introverted impression. In Kahn's design, the bookcase becomes a high wall behind which one feels secure. Opening the two ventilation panels, however, suddenly transforms the character of the room. The keyhole window appears, one can look through the high, narrow "loophole" toward the outside and fresh air comes in. Kahn could have installed normally opening glazing behind the ventilation panels.

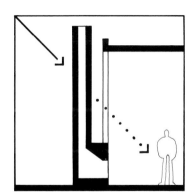

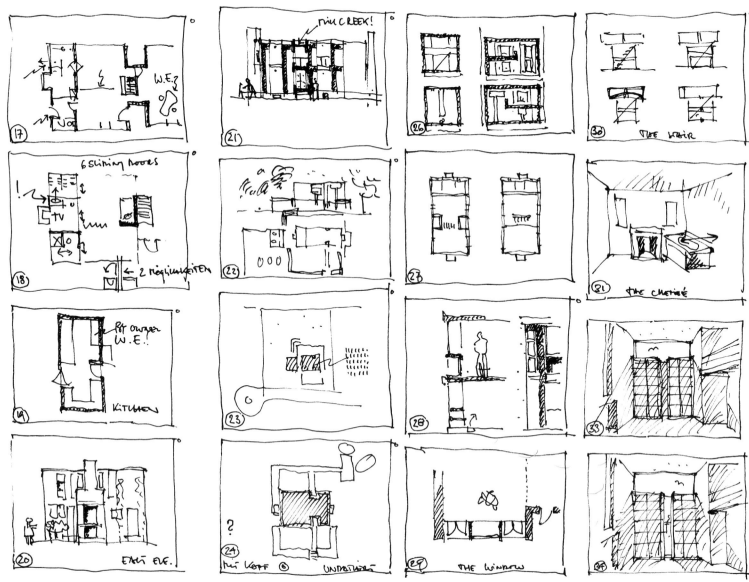

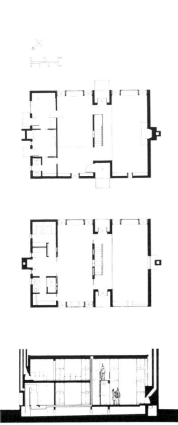

This would have granted the additional freedom, during winter, of providing the same transparency as in summer but would have implemented a certain indifference in the house to the seasons of the year. With Kahn's solution, on the other hand, man and his dwelling naturally adjust to the annual march of the seasons. In winter, one hibernates, so to speak; in summer, one opens oneself to nature. In the bedrooms, Kahn has additionally installed small, supplementary ventilation panels at the center axis of the windows. During the cooler seasons, they allow finely regulated cross-ventilation. Two fireplaces in the Esherick House provide both "night light" and warmth: one at the south wall of the living room, and the other in an upstairs bathroom. There, you can lie in the bathtub and enjoy a real chimney fire (analytical sketches no. 18 and no. 31). By means of a large wooden drawer which moves horizontally into the wall, this bathtub converts into a sofa. The house is heated by a sophisticated hot-air system which, however, does not function as air conditioning in summer.

Louis I. Kahn designed two further projects for the Esherick Family: the unbuilt addition to the existing M. Esherick House, and the atelier constructed for the artist Wharton Esherick.

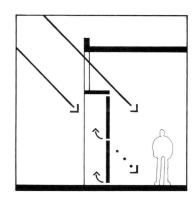

East facades
Analytical drawings
Ground floor; top floor; section
Northwest facade
Planned addition
Living room (with ventilation panels open)

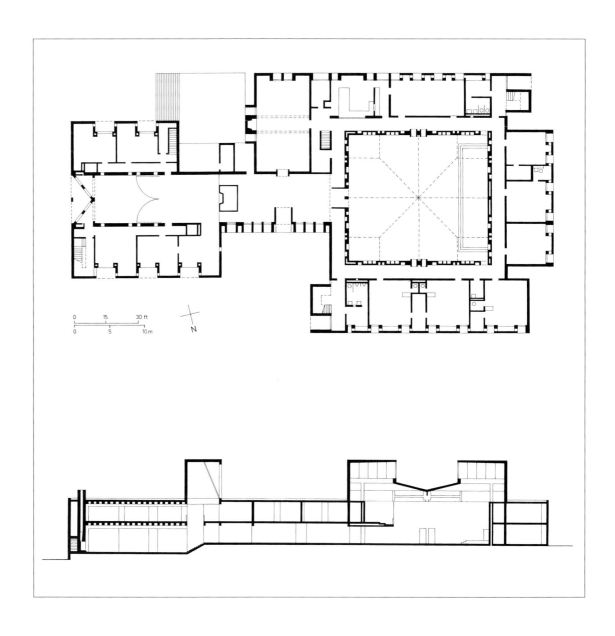

The First Unitarian Church and School was built in two stages. The first phase implemented the west wing with large sanctuary, classrooms in a peripheral configuration, reception room, kitchen, and library. Construction of the east wing followed as second stage. The differences between the two stages are clearly evidenced in the facades and floor plans. Kahn perhaps decided for the inwardly stepped brick wall on the basis of his visit to the Cathedral of Albi in southern France in 1959.

The plan of the large sanctuary is based on an almost perfectly square form. The roof structurally rests on the inside walls of the classrooms. The circumferential corridor for the classrooms is accommodated behind a 6-meter-high wall of concrete blocks. Four great skylights in the corners of the sanctuary admit light into the otherwise windowless room. The atmosphere in its interior therefore changes according to the height of the sun, the weather, and the seasons. For the first time, Kahn achieved success with a windowless interior room illuminated only by natural light falling from above. "It's very Gothic, isn't it? Does that bother you? I like it myself." (16)

The facade of the west wing with its pronounced three-dimensional modulation is a further logical development of the Morris House. The window niches are closed off above by terra-cotta tiles: the window glass is accordingly installed at the inside plane of the walls. In schematic drawings by Kahn, the footing areas in the

Plan
Section
Southwest facade
West facade

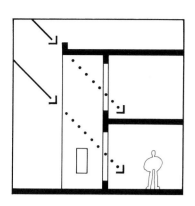

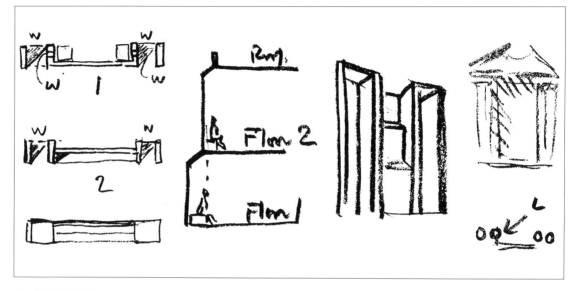

Explanatory sketches
Detail of window
on ground floor
Window niches
Interior
Light tower

window niches and the wall setbacks above the ground floor have been set off at an oblique angle. As actually constructed, however, the angles are straight. The east wing built years later also features window niches, although they are less delicately designed than those in the west wing; instead, they have been reinterpreted as giant "light ports." The east facade has one niche in which the window is hung in a V-arrangement. An essential principle here is the concept of using wall niches for protection of windows from direct sunlight and the elements. The window consequently becomes an architecturally articulated element, rather than merely an opening in the wall. Kahn writes:

"We felt the starkness of light again, learning also to be conscious of glare every time ... whether it's the glare in Rochester or glare in Luanda, it still was one realization.... If you looked at a Renaissance building ... in which a window has been highly accentuated architecturally ... a window that's made in this form... windows framed into the opening.... This was very good because it allowed the light that came in on the sides to help again to modify the glare." (17)

Also noteworthy are the small windows in the sides of the niches on the ground floor. They allow one to sit protected in the niches and "to keep a lookout" toward the outside.

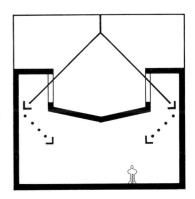

U.S. CONSULATE AND
RESIDENCE
1959 – 62; UNBUILT
LUANDA, ANGOLA

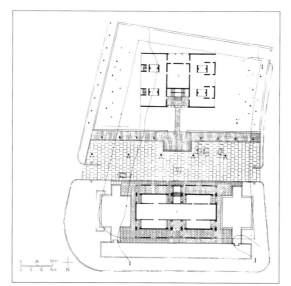

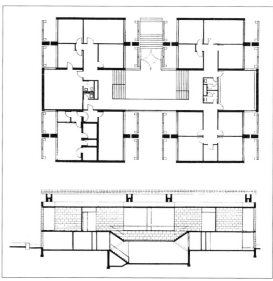

Site plan
Plan; section
Model
Axonometric projection
Explanatory sketch

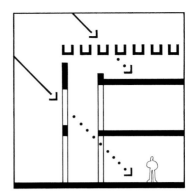

"I am doing a building in Africa which is very close to the equator. The glare is killing: everybody looks black against the sunlight. Light is a needed thing, but still an enemy." (18)

Distinctive for these two buildings on one plot are the brisesoleil walls in front of the glazed areas, and the newly developed sunshade roof. The administration building on the south side of the plot is formally and structurally more logically consistent than is the residential wing to the north.

The east and west facades are each protected by four freestanding concrete slabs (cf. the Fisher House). The north and south sides consist of windowless walls divided by the deep setback of the entrance. The eight pillars which support the sunshade roof are completely independent of the building itself: with the advantage that no pillars penetrate the roof surface of the office wing. Until now, this project represents the most logically consistent of Kahn's designs with respect to successfully thinking through solutions for problems such as directly incident sunlight, visual relationships between inside and outside, and protection from the elements. Although Louis I. Kahn later actually executed buildings under similar climatic conditions, he strangely never resorted again to this concept of a sunshade roof.

"I feel that in bringing the rain roof and the sun roof away from each other, I was telling the man on the street his way of life." (19)

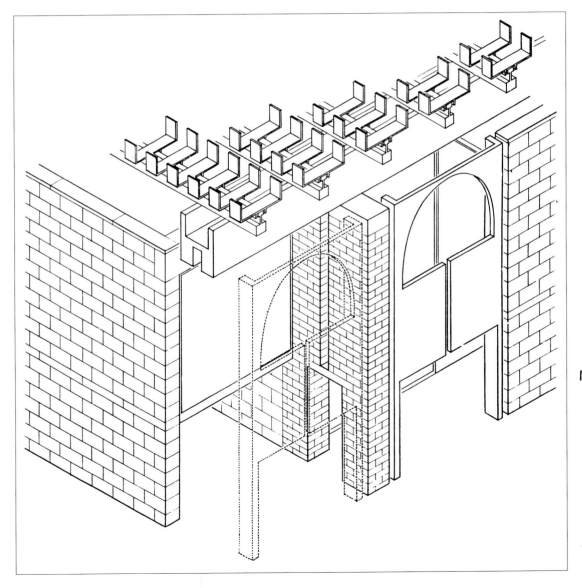

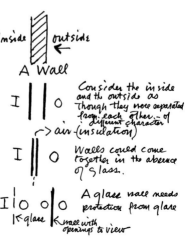

SALK INSTITUTE FOR
BIOLOGICAL STUDIES
1959 – 65;
LABORATORY BUILT
LA JOLLA, CALIFORNIA

Plan; section
Court
Picture of the model
Southwest facade

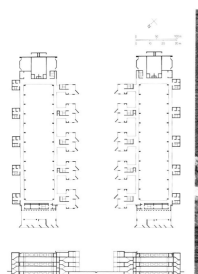

The plot of the research institute lies on the edge of a cliff which descends steeply to the Pacific. Of the originally planned three complexes, only the laboratories were built: the conference center and the residence for scientists were never executed. The two oblong buildings for the laboratories are arranged such that an open space is formed between them and the ocean: a space hardly equalled for splendor anywhere. Kahn's design for the research institute was originally based on the tower principle (cf. the Richards Medical Research Laboratories). Experience gained with the functional and lighting problems encountered with the tower constructions in Philadelphia, however, led Kahn to new insights and to a completely new solution in La Jolla.

Kahn once again employed Vierendeel techniques here, for a special room reserved for the media: but in this case, with such generous dimensioning that the occupants in this room have no difficulty in walking fully upright. The result is a room, without columns, which successfully ensures the required flexibility. Kahn provides for finishing of the unoccupied rooms resulting here to furnish floor space for service functions; the cantilever solution implemented for this space protects the glass walls of the lower-lying laboratory rooms from direct sunlight. In the scientists' study cubicles situated toward the ocean, and in the library rooms, Kahn installed horizontally sliding wooden panels in a novel manner (cf. the design for the Solar House). These sun-

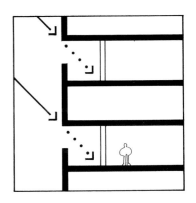

Plan
Perspective (late version)
Model
Explanatory sketch
Library (early version)
Library; pictures of the model

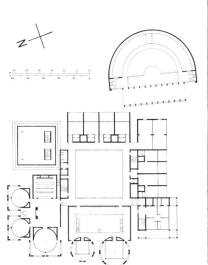

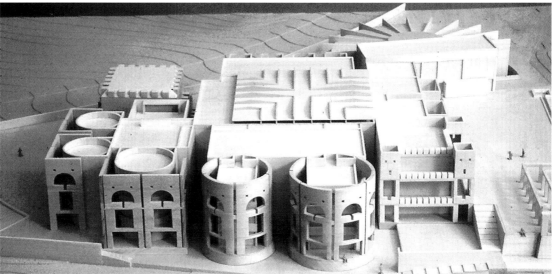

shade elements feature panels which can be adjusted as the occupant wishes. To provide ventilation, one can horizontally slide the entire window frames; the same is possible for the mosquito screening.

The design of the Meeting Place, intended for the northwest of the plot, resembles a cloister. This complex includes auditorium, guest accommodations, kitchen with dining rooms, seminar rooms, library, and a garden for strolling. The freestanding, fully glazed day rooms in front of the library and the dining rooms are protected from sunlight by a shell of "sun walls" (cf. U.S. Consulate and Residence). On a sketch, Kahn elaborated on this architectural solution for rooms confronted with the problem of glare. The semicircular openings cut out of the concrete shells diffract the directly incident light, allow a view of the outside, and cast ornamental shadows.

"I came to the realization that every window should have a free wall to face. This wall, receiving the light of day, would have a bold opening to the sky. The glare is modified by the lighted wall, and the view is not shut off. In this way, the contrast made by separated patterns of glare, which skylight grilles close to the window make, is avoided." (20)

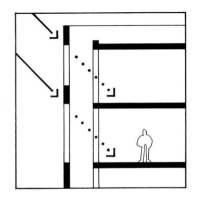

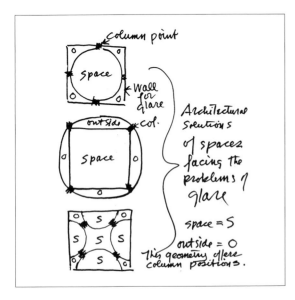

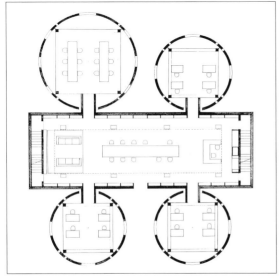

PERFORMING ARTS
CENTER
1959 – 73; BUILT
FORT WAYNE, INDIANA

"Natural light is the only light that makes architecture." (21) Nevertheless, Louis I. Kahn also excelled in the design of legitimate and motion-picture theaters, lecture halls, and other auditoriums, i.e., rooms with artificial illumination. Engineering alone can influence the character lent by light to such rooms and not the seasons, the height of the sun, or passing clouds. Here it is not fire as the "light of the night" which Kahn seeks to harmonize: rather, he addresses its modern counterpart, technical light, with the same thoroughness. Kahn demonstrated great sovereignty in handling of artificial light (cf. Weiss House, Yale University Art Gallery, Erdman Hall, and the Yale Center for British Art). Control of static artificial illumination is hardly comparable, however, to that of dynamic natural light. This project is merely representative of Kahn's expertise with artificial illumination, an aspect of his work worthy of treatment by itself.

The entrance facade may be interpreted as an overdimensioned symbol for the antique dramatic mask (eyes, nose, and mouth). Before and after evening theater performances, the coming and going of theatergoers is projected toward the outside as in an illuminated show window (cf. Kahn's design for the Raab Dual Movie Theater, not documented here). Behind this initial, extroverted envelope is the autonomous theater auditorium and stage, detached both acoustically and structurally from the outer shell: "the box in the box." The hollow

South facade
Foyer
Detail foyer

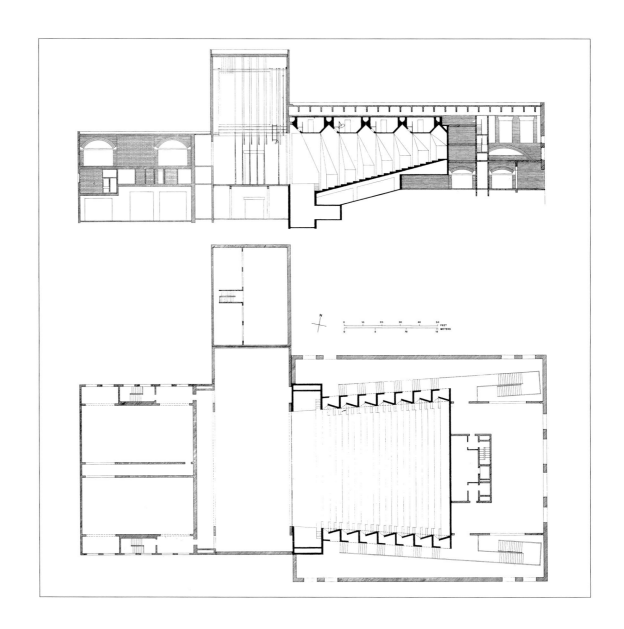

**Plan and section
Theater auditorium**

space in the ceiling accommodates the spotlights and the ventilation system, accessed via catwalks. The concept for the catwalks calls to mind the media rooms in the Richards Medical Research Building and the Salk Institute.

The auditorium is structured like a violin: the exterior brick shell is separated from the auditorium, like the carrying case from the violin inside. The oblique angles fulfill multiple purposes: a structural, a functional in that they form light bridges, and (not least) an acoustic function.

It is noteworthy that Louis I. Kahn worked on this project for 14 years, during which financial constraints extensively reduced its scope.

E.D. ERDMAN HALL
1960 – 65; BUILT
BRYN MAWR COLLEGE;
PENNSYLVANIA

Plan
Section
Top view of the roof
Foyer
Light tower

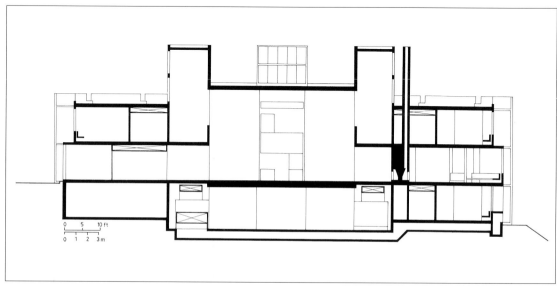

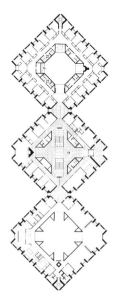

During the 1960's Kahn often referred to the Scottish castle Comlogan in Dumphriesshire to clarify his concept of a central common area with a pronounced periphery of smaller rooms. At Bryn Mawr, Kahn's design, as with the First Unitarian Church, is strongly based on a central courtyard surrounded by rooms. Twelve large towers admit sunlight into the central space of the three square constructions, which intrude into each other at two corners. Unlike the church in Rochester, the skylight glazing is oriented toward the outside a configuration which allows, from the ground floor, a direct view of the sky. Since light is not diffracted in the light shafts at all times of day, an excessive sacred atmosphere cannot prevail.

The inset facade creates the impression of a citadel. A kind of merlon closes off the vertically oriented top-floor windows. In the rooms extending beyond the inset facade, the window openings are installed laterally. When one enters one of these rooms, the view out is initially blocked by the wall installed on the central axis; the light niches to the left and right, however, make a correspondingly greater impression. The rooms one layer deeper in the building are illuminated by inset central windows. Rolling fabric shades installed inside the windows furnish protection from the sun. Surprisingly, the windows open only toward the outside, by a crank; when opened, they are exposed to the elements.

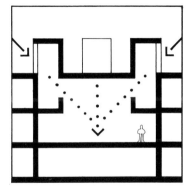

PHILADELPHIA
COLLEGE OF ART
1960 – 66; UNBUILT
PHILADELPHIA,
PENNSYLVANIA

Plan (late version)
Top view of the model
(late version)
Section of the model
(early version)
Explanatory sketch

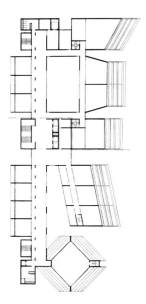

The Philadelphia College of Art planned to expand its midtown facilities, located on a block of Broad Street. The College intended to retain three existing buildings there, built by the architects Furness, Hewitt, and Haviland in the nineteenth century. Complex and extensive space requirements forced Louis I. Kahn to plan high-rise buildings to coexist with the old construction. The remaining open space was so small that Kahn designed special patios, or what he called "inside gardens."

The plans and the model pictured here are not fully identical. The floor plans represent the last version, in which the large central courtyard is rectangular. The models shown here are early versions which illustrate Kahn's concept of admitting light down into the center of the buildings. The huge light shafts which Kahn planned provide natural light to the classrooms and corridors oriented to the south, and additionally admit light through triangles cut out of half cylinders from the rear into the ateliers. Studios for the painters, sculptors, architects, and other artists optimally receive neutral, uniform light owing to their orientation to the north. The glass surfaces, some of them installed at an angle, successfully satisfy the expectations held by such artists for light characteristics. Kahn placed great emphasis on the visual contacts provided while walking through the buildings, and on the ability to see the students at work in their studios.

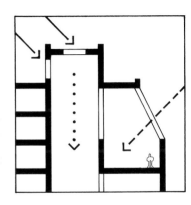

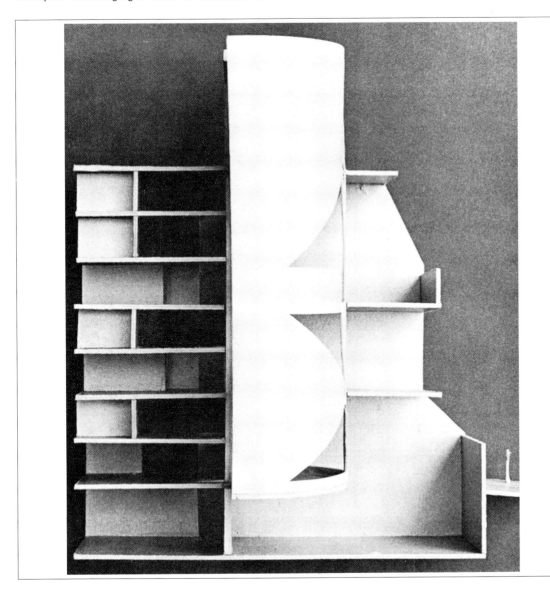

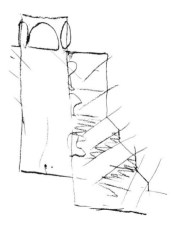

Ground floor; top floor
Southwest facade
Living room
Detail of window and
ventilation panel

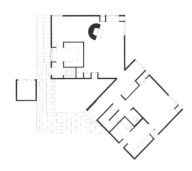

Louis I. Kahn spent six years on the design for this home, with surprising results from a number of viewpoints. As before, Kahn works here with geometric forms rotated at unusual angles to each other. He also follows the principle of distinct separation of the communal two-story living and dining areas from the private bedroom space, one primary reason being location of the living and dining room parallel to a brook, and bedroom orientation exactly in an east-west direction. Here, the corner window (also cf. Oser House and Roche House), together with the wooden ventilation panels and built-in bench, become almost a sculptural entity. This window extends over two stories, up to the ceiling, and provides a wonderful view onto the park-like yard. The corner window thereby becomes a panorama window. With the exception of three vertical light and ventilation slots, the facades toward the street are closed. The water-drip molds, horizontally slightly staggered, arrange the facade almost in the manner of a Mondrian picture. The non-opening windows and the separate ventilation panels are installed in the niches (cf. Esherick House). Along the east facade, the non-opening windows, the ventilation panels, the table, and the wardrobe chest in the two upper-story bedrooms are harmoniously integrated to form one great, multifunctional piece of "furniture." The wall as three-dimensional filter between indoors and out has been ideally realized.

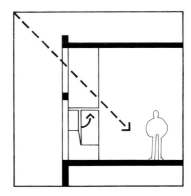

MIKVEH ISRAEL
SYNAGOGUE
1961 – 72; UNBUILT
PHILADELPHIA,
PENNSYLVANIA

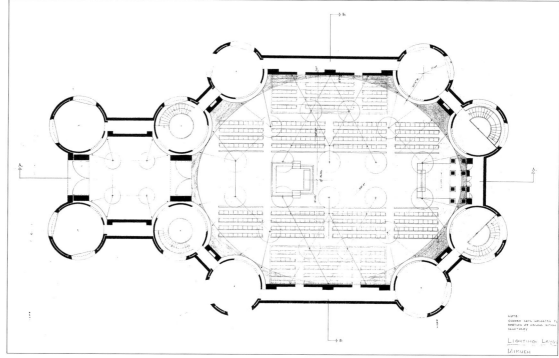

Louis I. Kahn labored on the design for this synagogue for over eleven long years. Complex space requirements were planned for realization in an historical part of Philadelphia, to include the synagogue (documented here), a chapel, a sukkah, an auditorium, a museum, classrooms, offices, and other facilities. Although Kahn's overall design was modified and reworked about ten times, the concept of the round "light towers" prevailed throughout. The floor plan shown here is from the seventh version, from 1964 - 1966, and is based on an elongated octagon in which an ellipse has been inscribed. Although Kahn's first sketches call to mind the Cathedral of Albi, the windows in this synagogue are in the tower cylinders, and not in the straight sections of wall.

A lens-formed ceiling structure with integrated joists spans the elliptical synagogue chamber and rests on the closed, straight wall slabs. This view of the underside of a ceiling, suspended over a room, is new in Kahn's vocabulary of architectural forms. The interior perspective depicts the underside of the ceiling as a smooth, white surface. If actually constructed, however, the wall openings would cast starkly pronounced patterns of shadow and light onto this surface. The impression created by the sanctuary ceiling is perhaps comparable to that of a canopy spanned over a public place. In his design for the Hurva Synagogue, Kahn further developed the concept of a sweeping ceiling to enhance admission of light into the middle of the room.

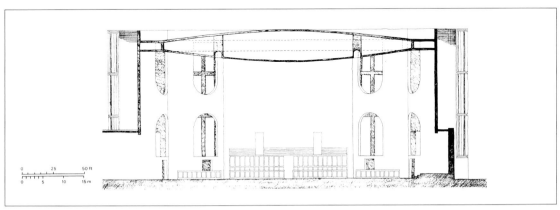

Elevation
Plan
Section
Interior

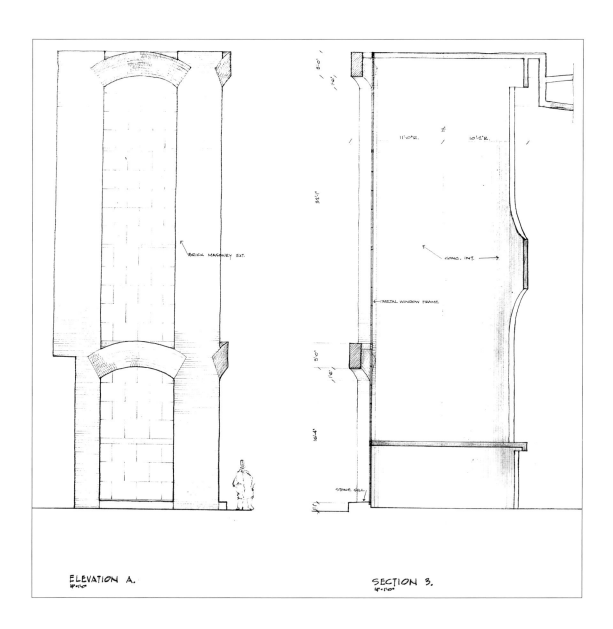

ELEVATION A.

SECTION 3.

What Kahn called the "light bottles" or "window rooms" additionally serve as a kind of joint or hinge for the entire space, and not only for illumination of the interior. The mighty light towers laterally accommodate the windows, which are framed by brick arches. Each cylinder is closed at the top by a concrete cover. The nonglazed openings at the inside of the towers admit light into the interior as through a giant filter. The wall surfaces therefore stand off dark against the light, with resulting amplification of the forms of the inner openings. The detail drawing of a light tower shows in the left view the window muntins; the section on the right depicts the glass surface detached from the cylinder form.

"The spaces are enclosed by window rooms twenty feet in diameter connected by walled passages. These window room elements have glazed openings on one exterior side and larger unglazed arched openings facing the interior. These rooms of light surrounding the synagogue chamber serve as an ambulatory and the high places for women. These window rooms prevail in the composition of the entrance chamber and the chapel across the way.... The windows on the outside do not support the building; what supports the building, as you can see on the plan, are the spaces between the windows."

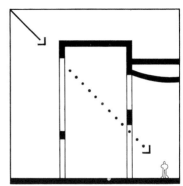

View and section
Light cylinder
Picture of model interior

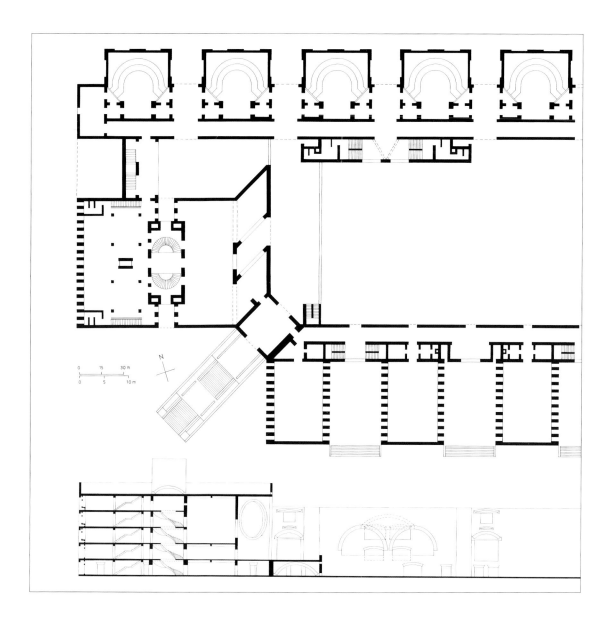

**Plan and section
Court
Explanatory sketch
(late version)**

Originally, B. Doshi was invited to design and build the Indian Institute of Management. Doshi, however, who had already collaborated with Le Corbusier in Ahmedabad, recommended Louis I. Kahn as architect. The design was prepared as a joint project, in the form of a studio assignment at the Institute of Design in Ahmedabad, and was further developed to the execution stage by Indian students in Kahn's office in Philadelphia.

Original planning was to build a complex on a flat area at the periphery of the campus, to include classrooms, offices, a dining hall with kitchen, a library, dormitories, apartments for lecturers, and staff accommodations. An artificial lake, designed to separate the classroom and dormitory area from the rest of the complex, was never executed.

"Sun-heat, wind, light, rain, dust": Kahn noted these five key words on 14 November 1962 on one of his first sketches. (23) These severe climatic constraints significantly influenced the Ahmedabad design over several years of planning and construction.

We may consider two individual buildings as examples for the entire intricate complex: the library and one of the dormitories. It is noteworthy that most of the buildings are oriented east-west, to benefit from the prevailing wind direction. The U-shaped building complex with classrooms, the library, and the administration facilities, was originally designed to be closed, like a cloister, around a courtyard. The dining room and the kitchen were later built on the southeast

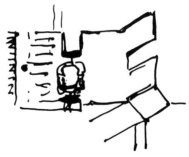

Interiors of the library
Entrance of the library

side of the site. Today, the entrance terrace, and the mighty screen including the "light and wind port" of the library, close off the square. The floor plan clearly reveals how the walls have been rotated out of the orthogonal geometrical pattern. These walls have been oriented into the wind (west to east), and modulate through three round windows the incident light admitted to the three-story reading room of the library. The feature of spatial depth zones and dual walls is clearly pronounced in this building. The wing walls set at angles are actually brisesoleils: not separate elements here, but integral constituents of the space as a whole. Kahn solved the problem of diffraction of the brilliant sunlight in a highly sophisticated

manner in this building. The round openings, seemingly punched-out, have become gigantically dimensioned parts of the architecture. The circular segments in brick are held in place by prefabricated concrete joists. Kahn amalgamates traditional brick with modern concrete to achieve a harmonic entity. The round windows in the library were originally open, but have since been glazed. This measure was a necessity, owing to powerful monsoon winds and to the coming and going of doves although the interior has lost much of its archaic impact.

The dormitories were designed such that the side walls of the two wings form a funnel, facing the wind, which provides effective ventilation of the Tea Hall.

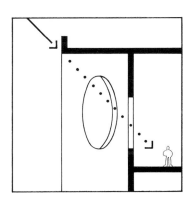

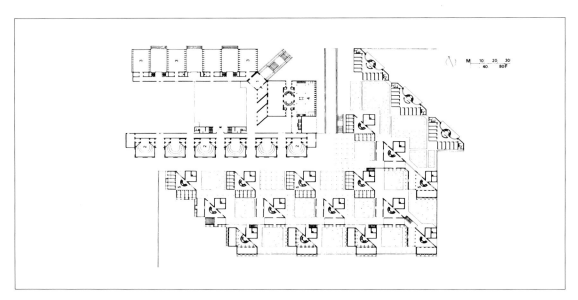

Window detail
Site plan
Plan
Dormitories

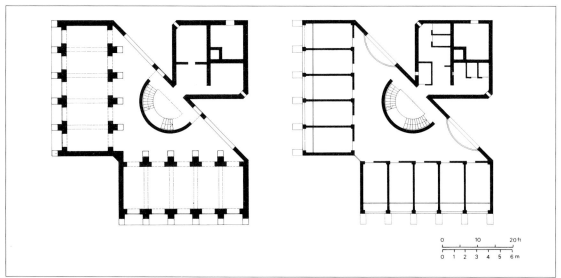

Adjustable ventilation panels below the non-opening windows permit regulation of room temperature. The ground floor contains the common rooms, above each of which are five students' rooms, arranged along two sides of the triangular floor plan. Balconies arranged in front of the rooms diffract the directly incident sunlight. The west facade contains huge round openings which provide cross-ventilation and allow a view from the common area into the shady inner courtyard.The kitchens and service rooms are connected, facing the west, like a backpack. The semi-circular stairway, located at the focal point of the triangular floor plan, dominates the entire building complex as light tower.

A ramp and bridge connect the dormitories to the school complex. Louis I. Kahn writes on his design: "So the system is fundamentally that of open porches. The exterior is given to the sun and the interior is where you live and work and study. The avoidance of devices like brisesoleils brought about the deep porch which has in it the cool shadow." (24)

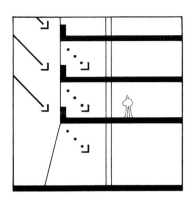

BARGE FOR THE
AMERICAN WIND
SYMPHONY
ORCHESTRA
1965 – 75; BUILT
PITTSBURGH,
PENNSYLVANIA

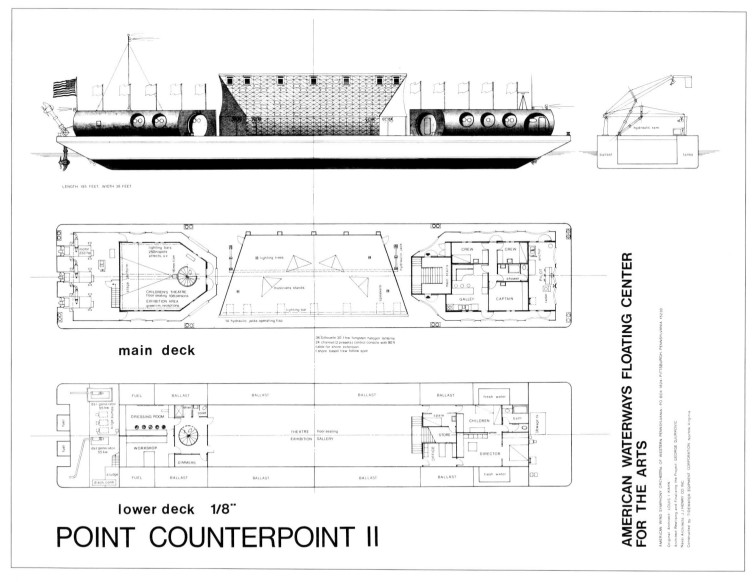

main deck

lower deck   1/8"

POINT COUNTERPOINT II

AMERICAN WATERWAYS FLOATING CENTER
FOR THE ARTS

AMERICAN WIND SYMPHONY ORCHESTRA OF WESTERN PENNSYLVANIA · PO BOX 1824 · PITTSBURGH, PENNSYLVANIA 15230
Original Architect: LOUIS I. KAHN
Architect Realizing and Finalizing the Project: GEORGE DJURICOVIC
Naval Architects: J J HENRY CO INC.
Constructed by: TIDEWATER EQUIPMENT CORPORATION, Norfolk Virginia

Louis I. Kahn designed two "concert ships" for the American Wind Symphony Orchestra of Pittsburgh. The first, modest version was put into service in London in 1961 and disassembled after the first concert season. The second ship which Kahn designed resembles in overall silhouette a coal barge, and features three diesel motors and all the navigation equipment required for full maritime operation. Since its completion in 1975, this barge has made concert stops in rural areas on the extensive system of rivers and canals in the USA. The deck accommodates the stage, cabins, and a small lecture room. The hull offers space for art exhibitions.

A roof designed as acoustic shell can be moved by two hydraulic rams over the orchestra stage. The form of a nautical porthole served as inspiration for Kahn in his design of the exterior skin of the ship. A slightly curved sheet-steel construction accommodates the lecture room and other spaces. Kahn had in earlier designs used the motif of circular openings (cf. Indian Institute of Management). As always with Kahn, the basic principle involved here is: provision of formal macroconfiguration for a nonglazed wall situated for the purpose of sunlight protection in front of finely structured space. The space between the fore-placed wall and the usable room serves for modulation of incident sunlight. The view outward from the barge is impressively framed by the round cutouts.

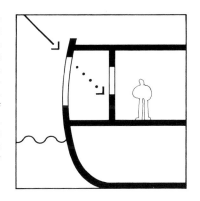

Elevation, plans, and section
Passageway
Barge

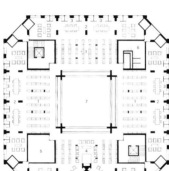

"Glare is bad in the library; wall space is important. Little spaces where you can adjourn with a book are tremendously important...." (25) These are, in Kahn's words, the three most important prerequisites for a library of which he admittedly fulfilled the last two in Phillips Exeter Library. I hesitate to say, however, whether he achieved a successful solution for the first. All four facades are identically structured; the entrance is on the north side. This highly imposing building, executed in brick and concrete, strictly follows the classical architectural rules for base, main order, and attic. The upward tapering of the piers of the external wall is also impressive here. The two-story windows, installed between the pillars, feature lower sections made of wood. The pairs of small windows illuminate reading niches; here, the reader can shut the sliding panels to close off the distraction of the view into the park, in order to concentrate fully on reading. Above the reading tables are huge sections of glass, installed without muntins, which are fully exposed to the sun.

"Originally, I had shutters on the larger windows. I feel still that shutters would be good on certain elevations. They didn't have to be on the north, and possibly would have been most advantageous on the west. This was not done because they can be easily installed at any time, and money was running out. The blinds were an equally good solution." (26)

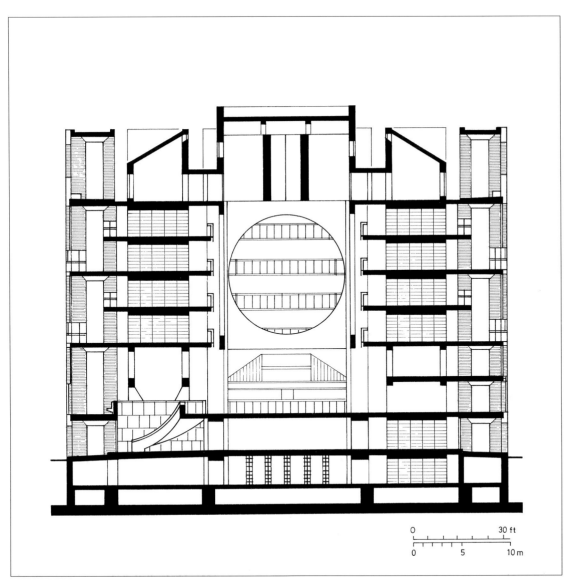

0   30 ft

0   5   10 m

Plan
Southwest facade
Section

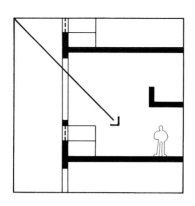

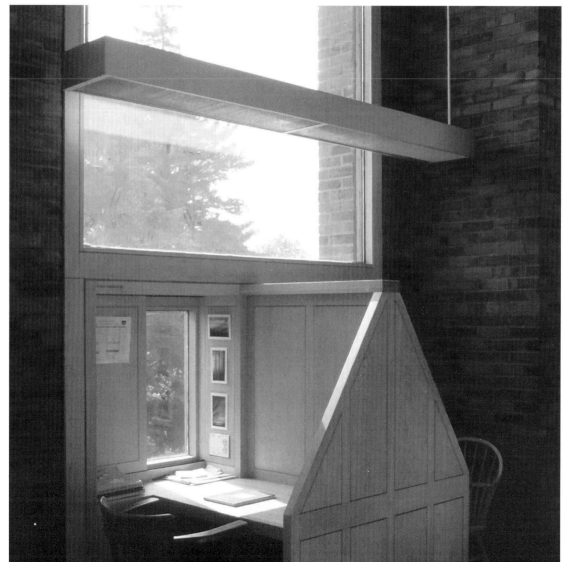

The section clearly reveals the depth-zoned configuration from the exterior inward: on the outside, the double-story edge zone of the reading area in brick, then the area of the stacks in concrete, and last the concrete core configured as an atrium provided with four huge circular cutouts in the walls. The cross diagonally spanning the square inner space serves to conduct the laterally incident light downward and to furnish an upward definition of this space. "In the central room I chose the kind of structure which shields the light so it is not pouring down." (27)

From the stairwell tower of the Yale University Art Gallery we are familiar with Kahn's principle of "light blades" which deflect light downward and simultane-ously perform structural functions. The diagonal position of the cross not only emphasizes the center of the atrium, but also renders definitely visible on the inside the border between main order and attic.

The four large circles cut out of the concrete slabs are best interpreted as windows not onto landscape, but into the world of books. Kahn's design therefore proves inviting to readers to select their book and take it into a reading niche or to the library fireplace to read.

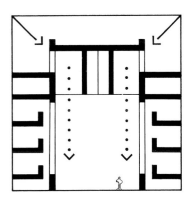

Reading niches
Central space
Light blades

OLIVETTI-UNDERWOOD
FACTORY
1966 – 70; BUILT
HARRISBURG,
PENNSYLVANIA

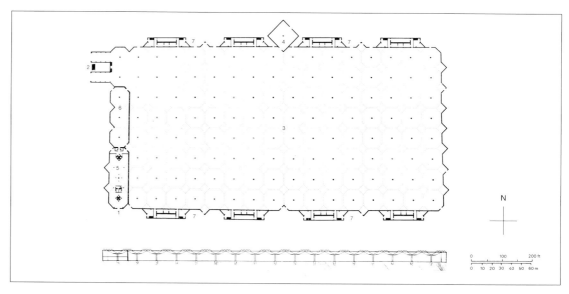

"In the Olivetti plant, the ceiling is a ceiling of light. Light looks right through it. It isn't as through it were covered. The light must be close to the work.... It is all open to view. Also the window in the Olivetti plant is above you." (28)

Design of the open-space room is based on a mushroom-construction principle. The columns stand in a square grid pattern. The contiguous octagon fields fit together to produce the square skylight which illuminates the interior. Tinted pyramidal roof elements of fiberglass ensure uniform incidence of light.

The facade is composed alternately of vertically configured concrete-block walls, and continuous vertical window strips. These glazed surfaces extend from the ground to the bottom edge of the concrete mushrooms and are shaded from direct sunlight by elements consisting of thin sheets of fine-meshed, black-coated steel. The sunshade panels stamped out of this material and bent to the horizontal are installed at close intervals to each other and go to make up a filigree brisesoleil. The interplay between light sources from the skylight and the windows is, however, not consistent at the periphery of the facade shell: there, two light sources directly conflict.

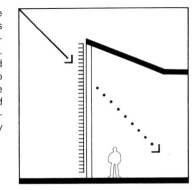

Plan and section
East facade
Window detail

133

KIMBELL ART MUSEUM
1966 – 72; BUILT
FORT WORTH, TEXAS

Play of light
Aerial view of the roof
Ground floor

"My mind is full of Roman greatness and the vault so etched itself in my mind that, though I cannot employ it, it's there always ready. And the vault seems to be the best. And I realize that the light must come from a high point where the light is best in its zenith." (29)

Louis I. Kahn was convinced from the very beginning that this museum should be built with a longitudinal arrangement. By 1969 he had produced four project versions. The floor plan is rectangular, with a deep niche cut out for the entrance area. Toward the west, the museum borders onto a park with its two open cycloid vaults at the periphery. The first impression gained from this construction is that of a simple structure based on repetitive implementation of one element. The north and south facades provide little hint of the magnificence in the interior. The massive concrete footing of the ground floor as well as the windowless external shell create a monolithic impression. Nevertheless, the structural design is in fact clearly evident from the outside: the supporting pillars cast in concrete, with the cycloid vaults resting above, as well as the non-loadbearing infilling walls consisting of travertine (and separated from the roof by a strip of windows). The cycloid vaults represent a structural engineering masterpiece. Each of these vaults rests on four pillars, and spans a length of approx. 30 m (104 feet), with the base sections serving as joists. At the crown of the vault, a slot-shaped opening has been made the entire length of the structure, to

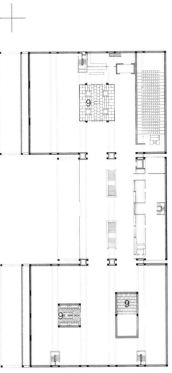

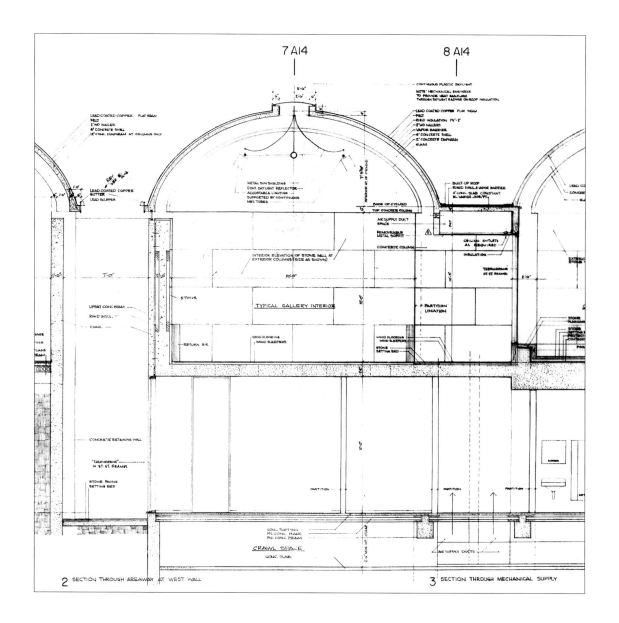

Section
Detail of natural light fixture
First lower story

admit light into the interior. Kahn installed crossbars to ensure stability at this point of maximum pressure and torsion. The edge sections become capable of supporting more loads at progressively higher points, in accordance with the increase of shear forces; as a result, tension rods are not necessary. Strangely, the plot of forces has not (yet) been entered on the detail plan here. The cycloid vaults were cast as concrete onsite, with smooth formwork. The interior surface of the concrete is only washed, and otherwise left rough. The cutting marks from the quarry have also been left untreated on the travertine surfaces.

Kahn attempted in countless sketches to develop an element which could be installed under the light slot in the crown of the cycloid vault to uniformly distribute the light throughout the room. He and one of his assistants found the solution after a long search: the desired light distribution was successfully provided by 50% perforated, curved aluminum elements with geometrical design calculated scientifically according to the angle of incidence of the sun. During construction, a full-scale prototype of this fixture was installed and tested for effectiveness: the final element ideally reflects and distributes the sunlight.

"This 'natural lighting fixture' ... is rather a new way of calling something; it is rather a new word entirely. It is actually a modifier of the light, sufficiently so that the injurious effects of the light are controlled to whatever

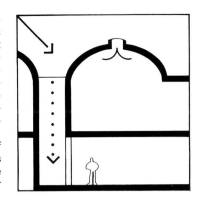

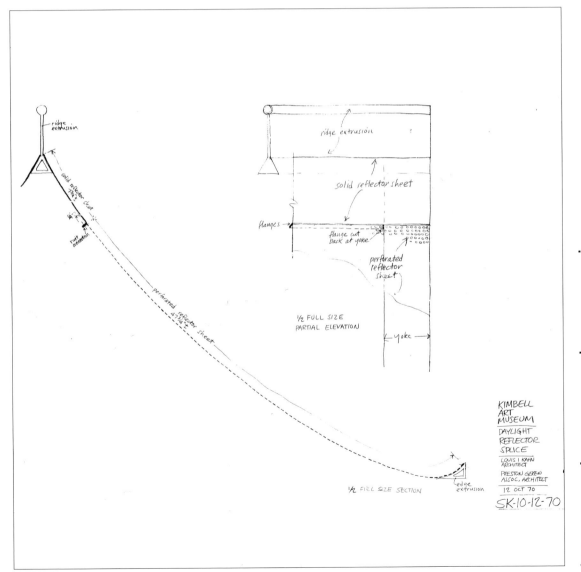

KIMBELL
ART
MUSEUM
DAYLIGHT
REFLECTOR
SPLICE
LOUIS I KAHN
ARCHITECT
PRESTON GEREN
ASSOC, ARCHITECT
12 OCT 70
SK-10-12-70

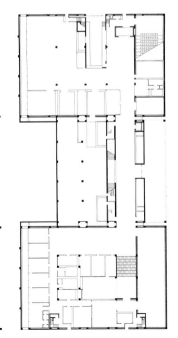

**Interior
Detail of a natural lighting
fixture**

degree of control is now possible. And when I look at it, I really feel it is a tremendous thing." (30)

The detail drawing shows how precisely Kahn designed each part of the "natural lighting fixture." The plexiglass-covered light opening at the apex of the cycloid vault is dimensioned in such a way that a particular quantity of light falls on the two blades for further distribution by reflection. The room therefore receives light not only directly through the perforated metal fixtures, but also indirectly as reflected from these blades and, in turn, from the cycloid vault. Flexible spotlights are installed at the edges of the "light blades" to provide additional artificial illumination. "An architecture must have the religion of light. A sense of light as the giver of all pres-ences. Every building, every room must be in natural light because natural light gives the mood of the day. The season of the year is brought into a room. It can even be said that a sun never knew how great it was until it struck the side of a building. When a light enters a room, it is your light and nobody else's. It belongs to that room. The Kimbell Art Museum uses all natural light." (31)

Kahn's self-criticism was well-known: indeed, he attempted to gain new insights from each project. In his own view, the Kimbell Art Museum represents one of his most successful buildings.

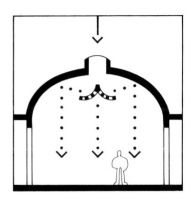

TEMPLE BETH-EL
SYNAGOGUE
1966 – 72; BUILT
CHAPPAQUA, NEW YORK

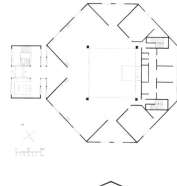

Kahn based his design on historical examples of synagogues executed in wood in Poland and Russia. The floor plan reveals an octagon shape, with four concrete columns supporting the "light tower." Kahn grouped the classrooms circumferentially around the synagogue chamber, as in the First Unitarian Church. In Chappaqua, however, there is no intervening corridor: one enters the classrooms directly from the central chamber (sanctuary). The reason: for well-attended events, the partition walls can be moved to the side to increase the capacity from 250 to 750. The sanctuary is paneled entirely in wood, which is integrated as infilling in the concrete skeleton construction. The light tower contains 24 identically large square windows, all installed without muntins. The architectural expression of this wooden tower, with the regularity of its windows, has been reduced to a minimum. The many windows allow the sanctuary to take part in changes of weather. Clouds moving past, sun, rain, twilight, and the like directly determine the character of this room to a degree which I had not experienced in other interior rooms illuminated by skylights. This impression may arise from the fact that the windows lie flush in the walls and therefore neither filter nor modulate the light. The air conditioning system compensates for the heat produced in the interior by the sun.

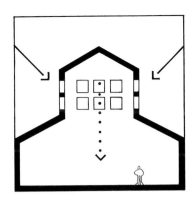

Plan and section
South facade
Light tower
Interior

HURVA SYNAGOGUE
1967 – 74; UNBUILT
JERUSALEM, ISRAEL

Plan
Site models
Models

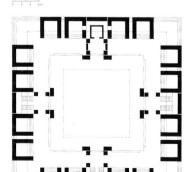

The old Hurva Synagogue was destroyed during the 1948 war. Today, a large stone arch marks its original site. It was only in 1967 that the Jewish community decided to plan a reconstruction. The Six-Day War and the Yom Kippur War, however, drained the necessary financial resources.

Hurva Synagogue is one of the mightiest works in the sense of massive power conceived by Louis I. Kahn. Pylons consisting of vertically layered stone blocks, each weighing tons, constitute the protective bulwark around the inner synagogue, itself constructed of light-weight concrete components.

"I sensed that the light of a candle plays an important part in Judaism. The pylons belong to the candle ser-vice and have niches facing the chamber. I felt this was an extension of the source of religion as well as an extension of the practice of Judaism."

Inside the protecting wall of sixteen pylons, the enclo-sure consists of a concrete shell which makes an upward-opening gesture. Kahn describes the concept behind the sweeping concrete shell as follows: "The construction of the building is like large leaves of a tree, allowing light to filter into the interior." (33) It is note-worthy that the flat roof is slightly lifted above the edge of the lower construction. If one looks up from the inter-ior onto the bottom surface of the ceiling, the roof slab appears to float, and the light falls softly downward over the curved shell. The plan sections clearly reveal that

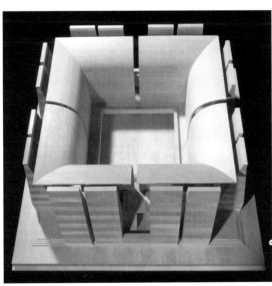

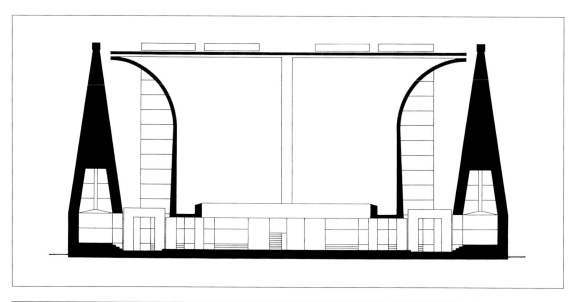

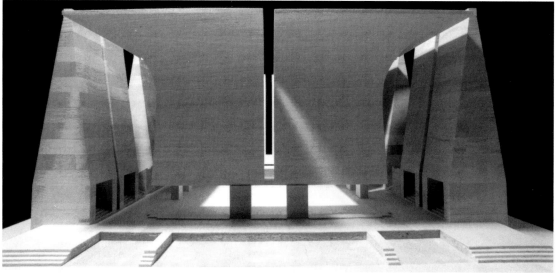

Kahn, by designing these massive protective pylons mounted in front of the seemingly fragile concrete construction at the heart of the synagogue, has in fact implemented a double filter for modulation of light. The concrete shell, opening upward like a flower, rests on eight relatively slender pillars arranged at the two center axes of the square. This configuration reinforces the impression which Kahn intended here: as though the room inside the mighty pylons has lifted and begins to hover. Vertical slots separate the inner concrete shell into four segments: as a result, direct sunlight falls for short periods of the day into the synagogue, and minimal outward glimpses are possible. The synagogue has four entrances one in each of the corners of the square plan. A circumferential ambulatory leads toward the inside of the building. Three stairways provide access to the gallery. Kahn's treatment of light and space for Hurva Synagogue demonstrates certain likeness to his work in Dhaka.

The special control of light in conjunction with the spatial qualities, the materials selected, and the formal and structural features make Hurva Synagogue one of the most beautiful and most distinctive designs conceived by Louis I. Kahn.

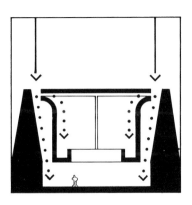

Section
Model
Light pattern

WOLFSON CENTER FOR
MECHANICAL AND
TRANSPORTATION
ENGINEERING
1968 – 77; BUILT
TEL AVIV, ISRAEL
SUCCESSOR ARCHITECTS:
J. MOCHLY-I. ELDAR, LTD.

N

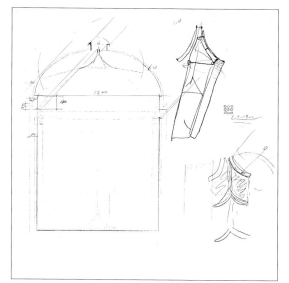

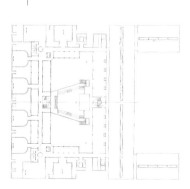

The Center for Mechanical and Transportation Engineering on the university campus in Tel Aviv is the only building which Louis I. Kahn actually built in Israel. Kahn grouped the extended oblong mechanical hall, the classrooms, the offices, and the cafeteria around a courtyard. He placed the auditorium as a lone building in the interior of the complex. Two annex buildings at the east of the site complete the facilities. Kahn's three halls here are strikingly reminiscent of his design for the Kimbell Art Museum. Kahn has likewise roofed these halls with cycloid vaults containing a light slot along their crowns. Light falling through the slot in the roof is distributed by "light blades" throughout the interior, as we have already seen in Fort Worth although the technical solution for Wolfson is simpler. In Tel Aviv, the natural lighting fixtures consist of aluminum strips mounted in a metal frame with reinforcing ribs. The aluminum strips have been precisely mounted to coincide with the required curvature of the overall blades. The incident light is reflected 100% onto the vault of the roof. Sources of artificial light are mounted at the underside apex of the reflector assembly. Kahn also installed slab walls in front of the classrooms to admit the dazzling sunlight indirectly into the rooms. The windows and the admitted natural light proved to be insufficient, however, with the result that the rooms must always be artificially illuminated.

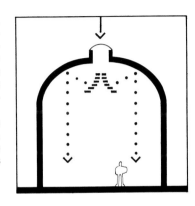

Plan and section
Sketch (late version)
Detail of light blades
Top view of the roof
Interior
Westfacade

YALE CENTER FOR
BRITISH ART
1969 – 75; BUILT
NEW HAVEN,
CONNECTICUT
SUCCESSOR ARCHITECTS:
M. MEYERS AND
A. PELLECCHIA

In two respects, the Mellon Center represents an exceptional project in Louis I. Kahn's late work. First, he executed the center as a pure concrete skeleton construction and, secondly, he for the first time successfully implemented stainless-steel plates as external cladding. Early in his work, to be sure, Kahn had attempted to employ this new mode of construction to develop designs of his own. His initial attempt, with the American Federation of Labor Medical Services Building, was plagued by conceptional ambiguities, problems which he definitively clarified and solved in New Haven. At the Yale Center, Kahn employs a regular column grid and replaces the Vierendeel joists plus floor slab as used for the Medical Services Building with floor slabs which contain interior cavities, and which appear at the facades on the exterior in their full thickness. Between the story levels, the sandwich constructions are visible, with stainless-steel slabs and protruding water-drip molds. The floor plan is broken down into sixty square fields, and is arranged around two atria. Originally, the square entrance court was planned to be open to the sky; later, however, on the basis of climate-control aspects, it was roofed over. In the second, larger atrium, a freestanding cylinder provides vertical access. The analogy to the staircase of the Yale University Art Gallery vis-à-vis is obvious, although this element is installed in open space at the Yale Center. Light comes through horizontally installed glass bricks in the roof slab of the concrete cylinder.

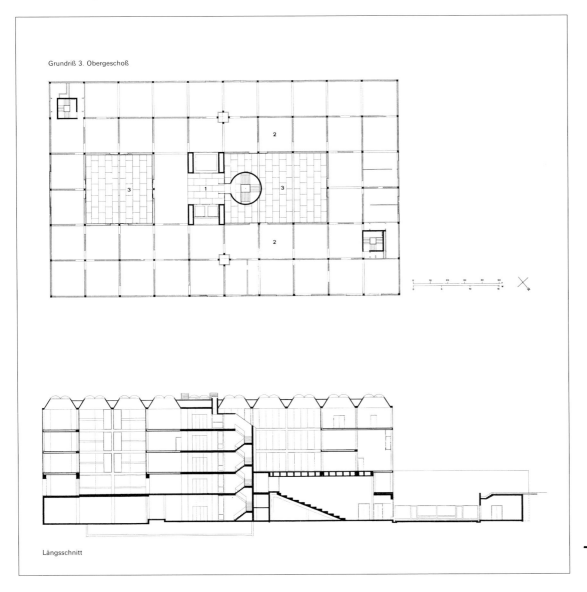

Grundriß 3. Obergeschoß

Längsschnitt

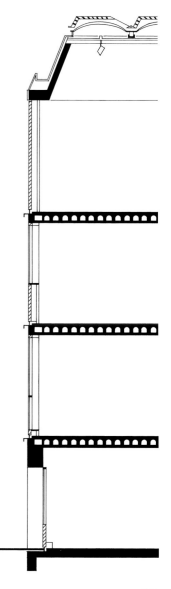

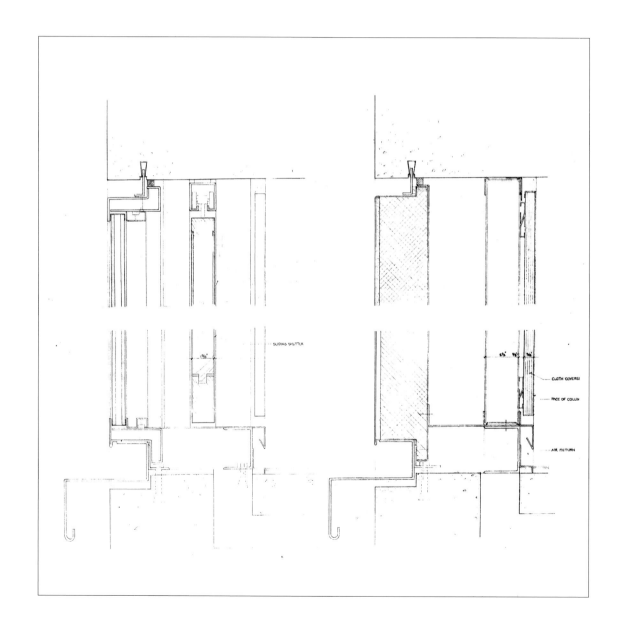

Northeast facade
Plan and section
Section
Detail of wall construction
(late version)
Interior
Sliding panel

In the facades, the windows are installed flush in the horizontally configured steel slabs. This arrangement together with the concrete pillars and the joists creates the impression of a smooth facade surface, structured only by the upward-tapering concrete members and the angular protrusion of the water-drip molds. Kahn integrates horizontally sliding wooden blinds into the wall construction to counter glare and directly incident sunlight (cf. design for the Solar House and the Salk Institute). Originally, fabric panels were installed: their use was problematic on formal grounds, however, and the wooden blinds were installed instead. Twenty-four years after he originally addressed the problem of protecting large windows areas from direct sunlight, Louis I. Kahn

implements here the perfect, coherent solution, in the form of the sliding blinds without protruding briseso-leils, without curtains, without special tinted glass, without overhanging roof elements, etc.

Skylights, covering the entire roof, illuminate the two interior atria and the exhibition rooms on the top story. Kahn installed sophisticated sunshades on the 58 skylight domes which, at all times of the day and year, primarily admit north light into the interior. These "sunshade caps" are the result of painstaking studies carried out by Kahn on all possible angles of sunlight incidence during the year. In order to obtain exact data on light quantity and quality, Kahn conducted trials with 1:1 wooden mockups of these sunshades, mounted on the roof of an existing

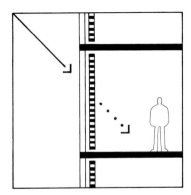

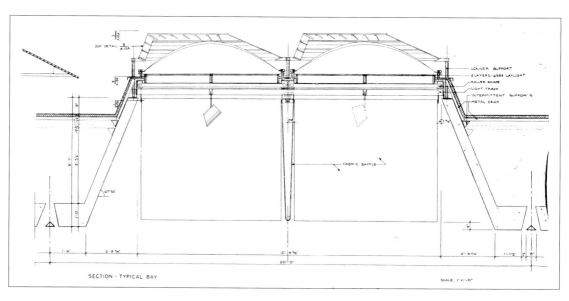

SECTION - TYPICAL BAY

SCALE: 1"=1'-0"

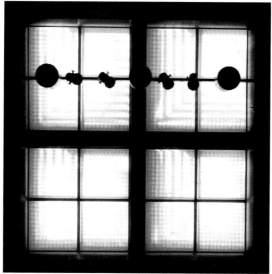

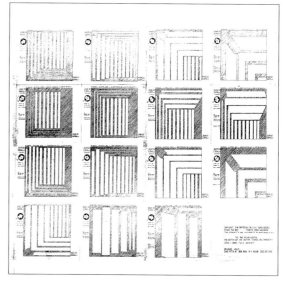

**Section of skylight
(late version)
Skylight
Shadow diagram
View of the roof**

152

building next door. He originally planned for adjustable panels made of flexible textile to better control the light (see detail section), but Kahn discarded this solution since the panels would have created space problems under the skylight domes. The 224 sunshade elements consist of a metal louvre construction resting on four support posts above the plexiglass domes. These sunshades present a relatively large shading surface toward the south, and the brisesoleil louvres below have been installed at the most effective angles to the incident sunlight. To ensure satisfactory admission of the light, the plexiglass domes rest in groups of four on V-shaped concrete joists (which contain ventilation ducts in their hollow interiors).

The skylights consist of the following components: two layers of corrugated plexiglass, one light diffusor with reflector coating, one clear plexiglass layer as dust protection, the inner ultraviolet-radiation-absorbing shell of the plexiglass dome, and the exterior shell of the skylight. Production considerations dictated that four domes be grouped to each skylight unit, which also contains spotlights for artificial illumination. Natural and artificial light therefore blend to a functional and formal entity.

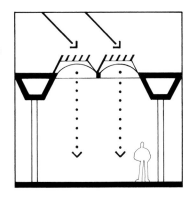

FAMILY PLANNING
CENTER AND MATERNAL
HEALTH CENTER
1970 – 75;
PARTIALLY BUILT
KATMANDU, NEPAL

Louis I. Kahn planned and designed the layout for intended public facilities on a triangular plot near the old King's Palace in Kathmandu. His master plan, however, was not accepted. Of the original H-form design for the Family Planning Center complex, only the south wing was executed. It is called "the house without a roof" in Kathmandu: originally, Kahn had planned to execute the terraces as roof gardens. Of all Kahn's late works, this project is most heavily indebted to classicistic sources. The columns reaching over three stories, together with the inset window units, endow the building with a monumental character apparently borrowed from the terminology of the Ecole des Beaux-Arts. The absolute symmetry of the floor plan, as well as the facade breakdown into base, main order, and attic, call Kahn's student work of 1924 to mind. The pilasters clearly recognizable in the floor plan with their U-forms serve to accommodate cabinets and vertical water and power supply lines. The window elements, executed in teak, are recessed along the inner column line, where they are protected from rain and sun. The wall as double structure is clearly in evidence here. The oblique angle of the base section in the window niches, as well as the parapet of the open top story, both create the effect that the columns appear longer and more slender. The verticality of the pilasters is broken up by the brick water-drip molds.

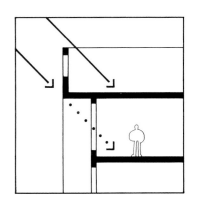

South facade
Window niche
Plan and section

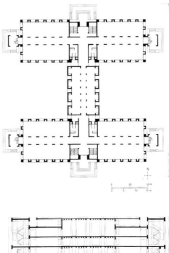

155

COMMON LIBRARY,
GRADUATE
THEOLOGICAL UNION
(GTU)
1971 – 77; BUILT
BERKELEY, CALIFORNIA
SUCCESSOR ARCHITECTS:
ESHERICK HOMSEY DOGE
AND DAVIS, AND PETERS
CLAYBERG & CAULFIELD

Section
Plan
Top view of model
South facade
East facade

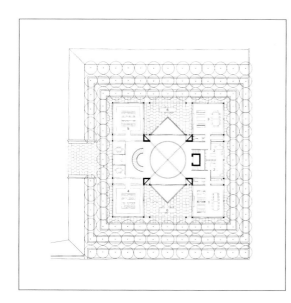

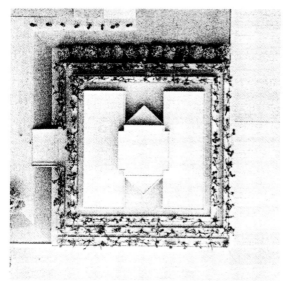

The clients specified that one large, single library be designed to serve Catholic, Protestant, as well as Jewish needs. The intention was to unite students of these religions under one roof and to offer them a common meeting place. This project calls to mind Kahn's design for the Washington University Library: in Berkeley, he likewise employs the stepped pyramid as dominant theme, but with a "green filter" instead of the sunshade elements planned for the Washington University Library. This filter consisted of trees planted in front of the windows: a concept employed here for the first time in Kahn's work. He originally planned to use orange trees, but climate considerations led to actual planting of 92 *Pittosporum undulatum* and 26 *Pittosporum tobira*

trees. At Berkeley, sunlight is admitted to the interior through a "light shaft." The configuration and construction of the "light blades" arranged in a cross is a further development of Kahn's system employed for admitting light into Phillips Exeter Library. The building actually executed in Berkeley by the successor architects deviates extensively from Kahn's original design, however. With the Common Library as originally planned, furthermore, a more satisfactory solution would have been achieved for the light problems resulting from the great depth of this building, difficulties with which Kahn had already struggled in similar form sixteen years earlier, in his design for the Washington University Library.

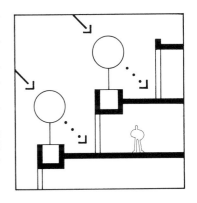

SHER-E-BANGLA NAGAR:
NATIONAL CAPITAL OF
BANGLADESH HOSPITAL
1962 – 69; BUILT
DHAKA, BANGLADESH

Plan
Sections
West facade
Portico

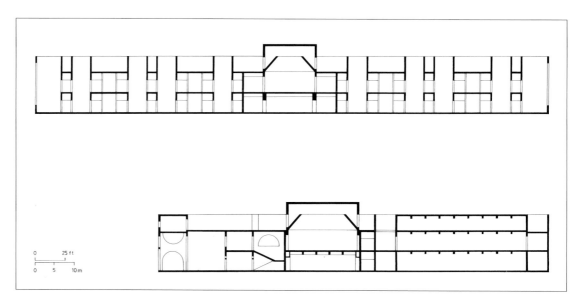

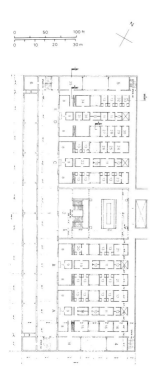

Of the entire large hospital complex originally planned, only part was built: the brick entrance section, the open waiting hall behind the entrance, and the examination and treatment wing. The portico, which stretches over the entire length of the hospital, consists of two spatial depth zones which diffract the sunlight and provide cooling shade. Giant circular segments have been installed in the first depth zone, perpendicular to the outer facade. The ceiling has been plastered in white and therefore helps to diffuse the light. Originally, the uppermost circular segments in the facade were not glazed. The concrete joists in the brick circles help to highlight the end of the portico as well as the middle section of the building. Kahn broke down the building into an even number of subdivisions (eight), in order to avoid placing an entrance on the axis of symmetry (off-set center). The second spatial depth zone is open throughout. A ribbed floor slab spans the long open area, from which secondary flights of stairs lead off to the left and right. In the large meeting room on the first upper story, laterally arranged concrete louvers reflect the light onto the ceiling, from where it falls in diffused and indirect form into the hall interior. This type of light modulation appears for the first time in the work of Louis I. Kahn, who shows us here again how he constantly struggles with the concept of light and its power.

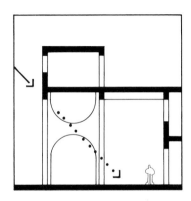

SHER-E-BANGLA NAGAR:
NATIONAL CAPITAL OF
BANGLADESH
ASSEMBLY HALL
1962 – 83; BUILT
DHAKA, BANGLADESH
SUCCESSOR ARCHITECTS:
D. WISDOM AND
ASSOCIATES

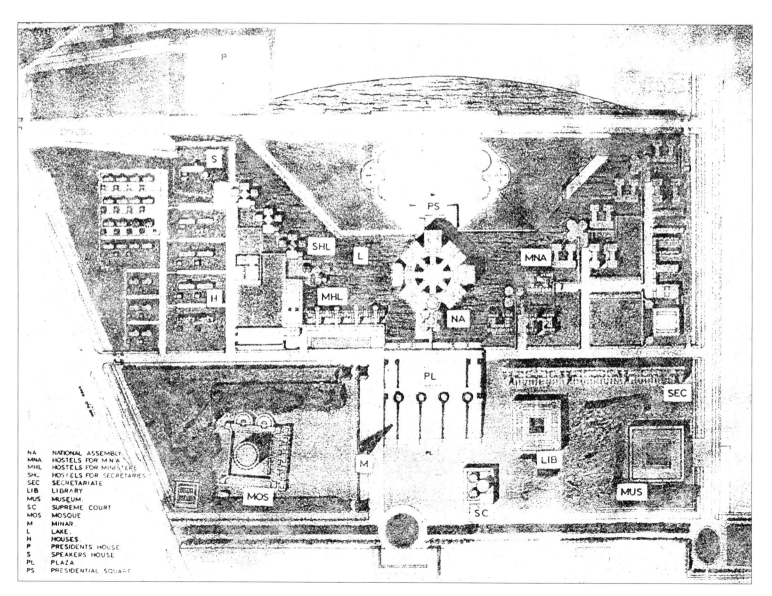

NA   NATIONAL ASSEMBLY
MNA   HOSTELS FOR MNA
MHL   HOSTELS FOR MINISTERS
SHL   HOSTELS FOR SECRETARIES
SEC   SECRETARIATE
LIB   LIBRARY
MUS   MUSEUM
SC   SUPREME COURT
MOS   MOSQUE
M   MINAR
L   LAKE
H   HOUSES
P   PRESIDENTS HOUSE
S   SPEAKERS HOUSE
PL   PLAZA
PS   PRESIDENTIAL SQUARE

In 1962, Louis I. Kahn was commissioned to design the executive capital in Islamabad (then West Pakistan, now Pakistan) and the legislative capital in Dhaka (then East Pakistan, since 1973 Bangladesh). The planning work was stopped in 1965 for Islamabad, but construction of the project in Dhaka was completed after Kahn's death.

The Assembly Hall is very well Kahn's most beautiful and most mature work. From the great variety of light-control and modulation techniques he employed in Dhaka, I have limited my consideration to the parliament building and to the hospital. The solutions employed for dining rooms, and hostels for government ministers, secretaries, aides, and guests are based on techniques familiar from other projects: primarily, the Indian Institute of Management.

"I was given an extensive program of buildings: the Assembly, the Supreme Court, hostels, schools, a stadium, the diplomatic enclave, the living sector, market: all to be placed on a thousand acres of flat land subject to flood.... I kept thinking of how these buildings may be grouped and what would cause them to take their places on the land. On the night of the third day, I fell out of bed with a thought which is still the prevailing idea of the plan. I made my first sketch on paper, of the Assembly, with the mosque and the lake. I added the hostels framing this lake. This came simply from the realization that "assembly" is of a transcendent nature. Men come

Site plan (late version)
South facade

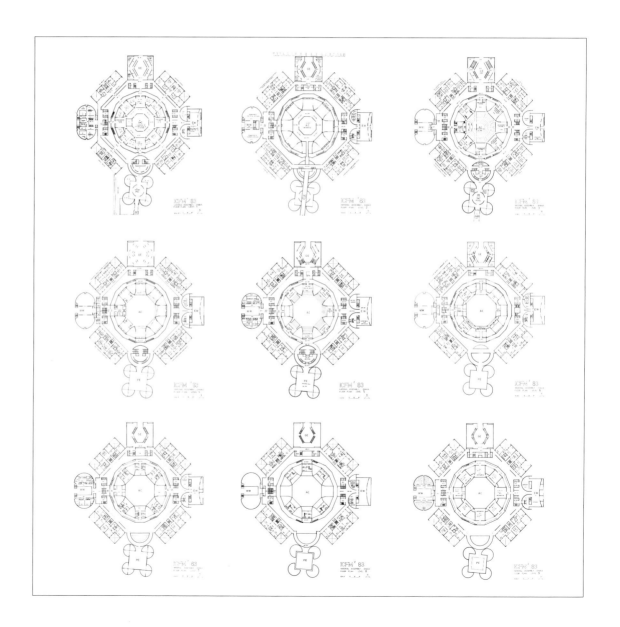

**Plans
West facade
Ambulatory**

to assembly to touch the spirit of community, and I felt that this must be expressible. Observing the way of religion in the life of Pakistani, I thought that a mosque woven into the space fabric of the Assembly would reflect this feeling. It was presumptuous to assume this right. How did I know that I would fit their way of life? But this assumption took possession as an anchor." (34) This first sketch contained all the essential elements of the complex. The parliament and mosque are set in the center, with hostels for government ministers and secretaries arranged in wings to the left and right, and separated by an artificial lake from the main building. The site plan shown here is merely a late version, since the final plan cannot unfortunately be published. Louis I.

Kahn rarely used the expression "the Assembly Hall": instead, he spoke of "the Citadel of the Institutions of Man." (35) The building indeed resembles a huge fortress. The fact that the building is surrounded by water and connected only by ramps and bridges to the mainland reinforces the impression of a fortification.

The plan clearly reveals the forms of the various building components around the Assembly Hall. The presidential entrance, with the diagonally arranged flights of stairs, is in the north corner. Prestigious rooms for government ministers face the west, and the mosque is toward the south, oriented to Mecca. Kahn located the great dining and meeting room to the east. Four office wings are inserted among these conspicuous elements.

A ring-shaped ambulatory, extending from the ground floor to the ceiling, circles the centrally symmetric Assembly room.

Upon entering this intermediate zone, one is overcome by the magnificence in the play of light. Sunlight, entering through glass blocks in the roof, flows like a stream of water over the walls and into the interior. The character and the atmosphere of the common space change with the daily progression of the sun.

The strip-configured glass blocks in the ribbed roof are mutually arranged at right angles: which makes even more interesting the play of light and shadows on the walls and floor. Since the inner shell of the office complex does not extend to the ceiling, the displacement between the light source and the visible sunbeams is clearly perceptible: the ribbed ceiling appears to float. The huge semicircles, circles, and triangles seemingly punched out of the walls flanking the ambulatory provide illumination for the corridors and staircases leading to the Assembly Hall and offices. Since these openings lie in shadows or in counterlight, they are endowed with even greater formal impact.

The stairways are located in a spatial shell inserted between the access ring on the ground floor and the Assembly Hall. These stairways pass as diagonals behind giant round openings which provide light to the upper levels of the Assembly Hall, small offices, TV and radio studios, and technical rooms on the top story. The

Glass blocks
Ambulatory
Light shaft
View of the roof
Ribbed floor slab

Play of light in ambulatory

inner access way is connected by bridges to the outside corridor on the east and west.

Eight wedge-shaped light shafts penetrate to the core of the central building. Their apices define the octagon of the Assembly Hall. These inner courts are glazed on three sides and hence permit illumination (and ventilation) of the adjoining rooms. Their design at the interior is purely functional. The eight huge vertical circles at the top of the building, however, distinctively characterize the imposing attic level. The light shafts are open to the sky. The use of aluminum window frames in the interior of the courts eliminates damage by the elements. This solution, the vertical admission of light, can also be found in the Philadelphia College of Art project (1960 - 1966).

The two office sections are designed as mirror images of each other, and are each set in an L-arrangement around a square atrium. The stairway complex with the foyer in front is illuminated by a recessed "slot window" extending over all stories. Each of the corners in which the light shafts are located features a rectangle, a vertical triangle, and a circle on the side. These openings allow a view toward the outside, and filter the directly incident light. The main source of light, however, is the roof of glass blocks over the atrium.

Originally, Kahn planned to leave this space open toward the sky. Owing to the severe monsoon rains and their effects on wooden window components, however, the decision was reached after 1974 to close off the

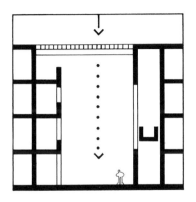

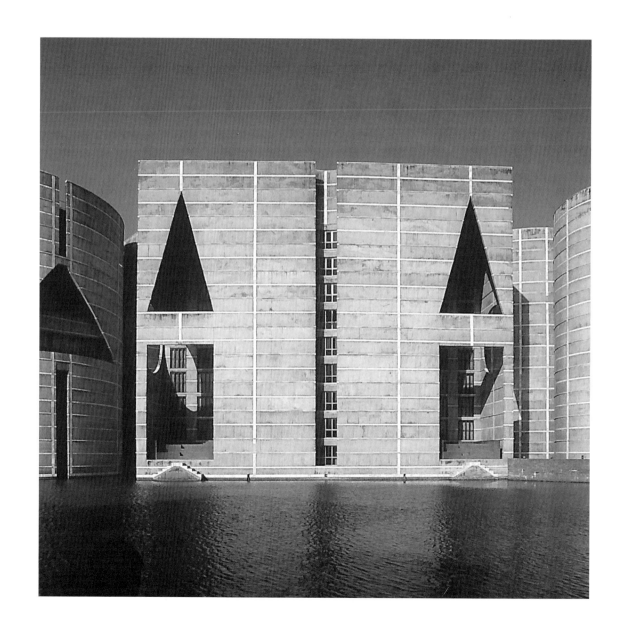

Office section
Atrium
View of the atrium

light shaft with transparent material. As a result, the light space here has lost much of its original architectural force.

A total of 128 glass blocks are installed in the square concrete ribs, resulting in the diffusion of sunlight and the even illumination of the office rooms.

The horizontal strips in the masonry mark the level of the concrete cast forms, at heights of five feet (a story here is 10 feet, i.e., about 3 m). The joints between the individual concrete pouring strips are inlaid with white marble. In the external facade, the height of the floor slabs is visualized by strips provided as water-drip molds.

Within the purely centrally symmetrical configuration of the Assembly Hall, the geometry of the mosque has been slightly revolved out of the north-south axis, in order to orient it exactly toward Mecca. The cubic interior is flanked by four "light cylinders."

The Prayer Room is characterized by absolute introversion, with no view of the outside: no windows, no openings, no loopholes, nothing except light falling from above. Seen from the outside, the towers with the entrance gate indeed call to mind a citadel. Considered from the inside, however, the interior design of the Prayer Room proves exceedingly complex and extraordinary indeed. Semicircles and full circles set-Unlike the offices, the light shafts here open to the sky. Wind and weather can therefore be experienced inside the mosque, and rays of sunlight variously enter the

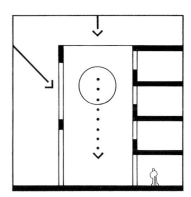

South facade
Prayer room
Light shaft

Prayer Room, depending on the time of day. Passing clouds strongly influence the character of the interior. Artificial light fixtures are hung low, in accordance with mosque tradition, to create a subdued, more intimate atmosphere during the night. The foyer beneath the Prayer Room is also illuminated by the four "light cylinders."

The very heart of the design for the National Capital is the Assembly Hall, the parliament chamber for the national legislative body, surrounded by its ring of "serving spaces": offices, ministers' offices, reception rooms, and TV and radio studios. The plan is based on an octagon covered by an umbrella-formed, vaulted roof. In 1964, Kahn wrote:

"In the Assembly I have introduced a light-giving element to the interior of the plan. If you see a series of columns, you can say that the choice of columns is a choice in light. The columns as solids frame the spaces of light. Now, think of it just in reverse, and think that the columns are hollow and much bigger and that their walls can themselves give light. Then, the voids are rooms, and the column is the maker of light and can take on complex shapes and be the supporter of spaces and give light to spaces. I am working to develop the element to such an extent that it becomes a poetic entity which has its own beauty outside of its place in the composition. In this way, it becomes analogous to the solid column I mentioned above as a giver of light." (36)

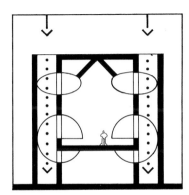

It is noteworthy that Kahn worked for many years to find a suitable solution for the roof of the Assembly Hall. His initial proposals proved to be unfeasible on the basis of engineering calculations, or they were simply too expensive. It was only in 1972, i.e., ten years after award of contract that he found a solution, in collaboration with the engineer Palmbaum. The final roof design is new and surprising in Kahn's work: an umbrella form (hyperbolic paraboloid) which spans the octagon of the Assembly Hall on extremely fragile-seeming support points. Kahn describes a new approach with structural concepts: the eight supporting "umbrella tips" of the hyperbolic paraboloid taper precisely at points of greatest loads. It is, however, not only these illogically downward-tapering umbrella tips which represented a structural-engineering problem: the drain pipes installed on the inside also posed difficulties. The marble strips in the vaulted roof are purely decorative: here, Kahn plays with an element which is a structural component in the facade construction.

The hyperbolic-paraboloid roof calls Renaissance buildings to mind. In the Assembly Hall roof, however, Kahn appears not to have succeeded entirely in his borrowing of solutions from architectural history forms which he subjected to a completely new form of interpretation. The archaic, ponderous, castle-like language of the Assembly complex seems to stand in contradiction to the fragile appearance of the vaulted roof.

North facade
Assembly hall

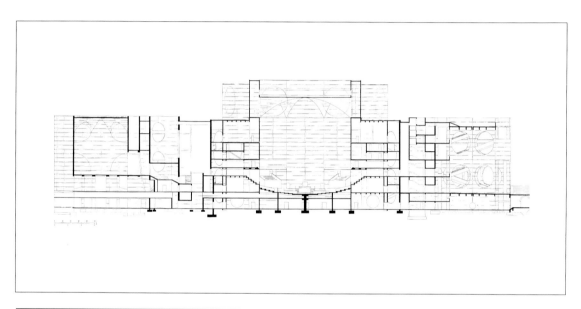

In Dhaka, a "ring of light" encircles the intrinsically floating paraboloid dome. The light is admitted from the side walls, through the parabola openings, into the interior. Above the dome, an inwardly oriented strip window is inscribed in the octagon, and the glazed surface is flush with the border of the dome. To provide more light for the Hall, Kahn originally installed additional, vertically slotted windows on the outside wall of the "ring of light." Owing to glare, however, they are now covered with white fabric strips.

Standing in the Assembly Hall, one is truly overwhelmed by the daring and by the magnificence of the architecture. The Assembly complex is indeed Louis I. Kahn's most fascinating and most beautiful work characterized as it utterly is by the idea of modulation of light. His achievements in Dhaka represent an architectural jewel of our age.

"The architectural image of the Assembly building grows out of the conception to hold a strong essential form to give particular shape to the varying interior needs, expressing them on the exterior. The image is that of a many-faceted, precious stone, constructed in concrete and marble." (37)

Section
Paraboloid roof
Assembly hall

Light space
View of the roof
Paraboloid roof

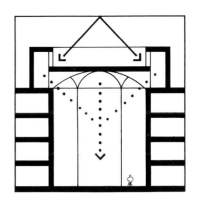

Architecture is the making of a room; an assembly of rooms. The light is the light of that room. Thoughts exchanged by one and another are not the same in one room as in another.

A street is a room; a community room by agreement. Its character from intersection to intersection changes and may be regarded as a number of rooms

Sketch by Louis I. Kahn

The chronological listing of projects traces Kahn's development process in light control and modulation. Projects beginning with student work from 1924 and ending with the Berkeley library from 1971-1974 reveal an extraordinarily broad spectrum of solutions for the design of light and space. Kahn's struggle to find the coherent answer for each architectural challenge remains the basic principle characterizing his complete work. Kahn did not fall back on received principles or rules, but saw each design as a challenge to start anew, from scratch. For him, the control of light and the structuring of space are indivisibly interwoven.

In his early work, Kahn installed the window as a simple opening in an ordinary single-shell wall. The brise-soleil and the canopy roof followed as logical steps in Kahn's development process, in efforts to better control direct sunlight. The concept of vertical sliding wooden panels occupied Kahn's attention for years, but was later discarded – as were his horizontal brisesoleils – in favor of distinctively innovative solutions. Double-shell walls offered Kahn the possibility of solving the problem of light control and modulation in his own, original manner. Kahn never ceased to further develop and to sophisticate these "light filters." Indoors and outdoors were then no longer divided by a simple wall with openings, as in his early work: the interface became multi-layer space in which light is modulated. Kahn placed these vertical light filters in front of the main facades, or

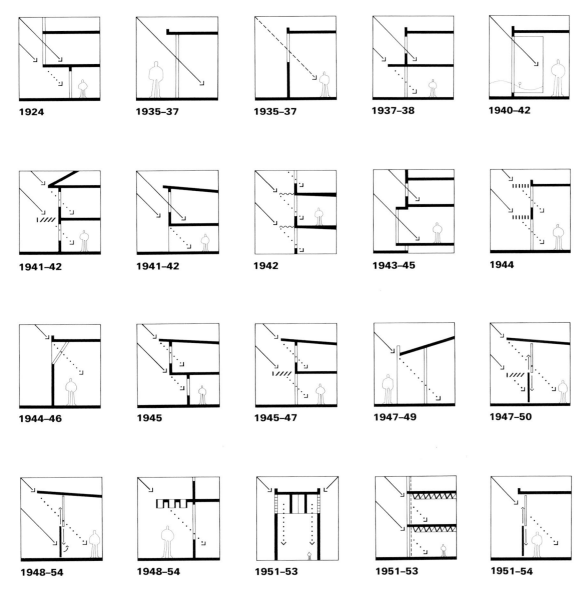

1924 1935–37 1935–37 1937–38 1940–42

1941–42 1941–42 1942 1943–45 1944

1944–46 1945 1945–47 1947–49 1947–50

1948–54 1948–54 1951–53 1951–53 1951–54

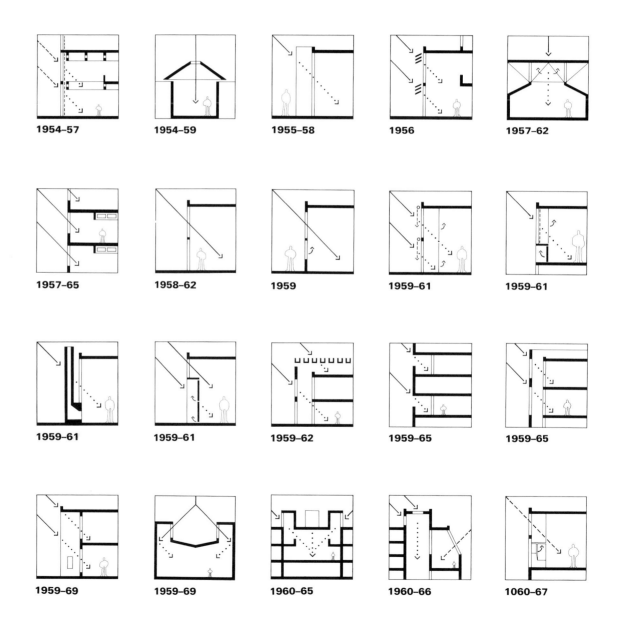

1954–57	**1954–59**	**1955–58**	**1956**	**1957–62**
1957–65	**1958–62**	**1959**	**1959–61**	**1959–61**
1959–61	**1959–61**	**1959–62**	**1959–65**	**1959–65**
1959–69	**1959–69**	**1960–65**	**1960–66**	**1060–67**

integrated the two elements; in his late work, these light filters increasingly took on archaic forms. "Light shields" featuring circular, triangular, or rectangular openings endow Kahn's architecture with its truly distinguishing traits. These interstices enable not only light modulation, but also provide ventilation and framed views toward the outside. Although Kahn did not employ the skylight as an element of illumination at the beginning, it became increasingly important for light control in his late works. Ranging from simple openings in a pyramidal roof, all the way to a complex dome structure, Kahn developed an astonishing spectrum of architectural solutions for skylight illumination of central as well as peripheral rooms. They have been arranged in this typo-

logy by chronological order according to the year of project award. Kahn's never-ending search for the optimal solution to a design problem is reflected in the fact that my analytical study extends to the year 1971, only three years before his death. A number of unbuilt projects follow during the period of 1971 to 1974, but their distinguishing attributes are not evident from the schematic representations available to us.

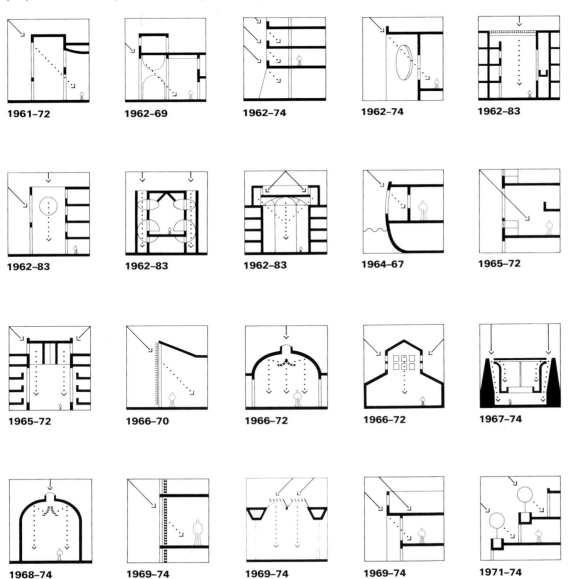

1961–72 1962–69 1962–74 1962–74 1962–83

1962–83 1962–83 1962–83 1964–67 1965–72

1965–72 1966–70 1966–72 1966–72 1967–74

1968–74 1969–74 1969–74 1969–74 1971–74

181

REFERENCES

1 Wurman, R.S.; Feldman, E.: The notebooks and drawings of Louis I. Kahn. (MIT Press, Cambridge, Mass., and London, England, 1973).

2 Wurman, R.S.: What will be has always been. The words of Louis I. Kahn; from a conversation with Robert Wemischner, April 17, 1971; pp. 121 (Access Press / Rizzoli, New York, 1986).

3 Wurman, R.S.: What will be has always been. The words of Louis I. Kahn; the white light and the black shadow, lecture at Princeton University, March 6, 1968; pp. 15 (Access Press / Rizzoli, New York, 1986).

4 Wurman, R.S.: What will be has always been. The words of Louis I. Kahn; from a conversation with Jaime Mehta, October 22, 1973; pp. 230 (Access Press / Rizzoli, New York, 1986).

5 Wurman, R.S.: What will be has always been. The words of Louis I. Kahn; the invisible city – International Design Conference at Aspen, June 19, 1972; pp. 153 (Access Press / Rizzoli, New York, 1986).

6 Wurman, R.S.: What will be has always been. The words of Louis I. Kahn; architecture and human agreement, a Tiffany lecture, October 10, 1973; pp. 215 (Access Press / Rizzoli, New York, 1986).

7 Wurman, R.S.: What will be has always been. The words of Louis I. Kahn; University of Cincinnati, College of Design, Architecture, Art and Planning; pp. 75 (Access Press / Rizzoli, New York, 1986).

8 Wurman, R.S.: What will be has always been. The words of Louis I. Kahn; the invisible city – International Design Conference at Aspen, June 19, 1972; pp. 151 (Access Press / Rizzoli, New York, 1986).

9 Wurman, R.S.; Feldman, E.: The notebooks and drawings of Louis I. Kahn. (MIT Press, Cambridge, Mass., and London, England, 1973).

10 Wurman, R.S.; Feldman, E.: The notebooks and drawings of Louis I. Kahn. (MIT Press, Cambridge, Mass., and London, England, 1973).

11 Wurman, R.S.: What will be has always been. The words of Louis I. Kahn; progressive architecture 1969, special edition, wanting to be: the Philadelphia school; pp. 89 (MIT Press, Cambridge, Mass., and London, England, 1973).

12 Wurman, R.S.: What will be has always been. The words of Louis I. Kahn; Perspecta 3, the Yale architectural journal 1955; pp. 2 (MIT Press, Cambridge, Mass., and London, England ,1973).

13 Wurman, R.S.: What will be has always been. The words of Louis I. Kahn; lecture, Drexel Architectural Society, Philadelphia, Pa., November 5, 1968, pp. 29 (MIT Press, Cambridge, Mass., and London, England, 1973).

14 Ronner, H.; Jhaveri, S.: Complete Work 1935 – 74; 2nd ed., pp. 65 (Birkhäuser Verlag, Basel, 1987).

15 Ronner, H.; Jhaveri, S.: Complete Work 1935 – 74; 2nd ed., pp. 83 (Birkhäuser Verlag, Basel, 1987).

16 Ronner, H.; Jhaveri, S.: Complete Work 1935 – 74; 2nd ed., pp. 122 (Birkhäuser Verlag, Basel, 1987).

17 Ronner, H.; Jhaveri, S.: Complete Work 1935 – 74; 2nd ed., pp. 120 (Birkhäuser Verlag, Basel, 1987).

18 Wurman, R.S.: What will be has always been. The words of Louis I. Kahn; voice of America; pp. 8 (Access Press / Rizzoli, New York, 1986).

19 Ronner, H.; Jhaveri, S.: Complete Work 1935 – 74; 2nd ed., pp. 128 (Birkhäuser Verlag, Basel, 1987).

20 Ronner, H.; Jhaveri, S.: Complete Work 1935 – 74; 2nd ed., pp. 134 (Birkhäuser Verlag, Basel, 1987).

21 Ronner, H.; Jhaveri, S.: Complete Work 1935 – 74; 2nd ed., pp. 344 (Birkhäuser Verlag, Basel, 1987).

22 Ronner, H.; Jhaveri, S.: Complete Work 1935 – 74; 2nd ed., pp. 189 (Birkhäuser Verlag, Basel, 1987).

23 Ronner, H.; Jhaveri, S.: Complete Work 1935 – 74; 2nd ed., pp. 208 (Birkhäuser Verlag, Basel, 1987).

24 Ronner, H.; Jhaveri, S.: Complete Work 1935 – 74; 2nd ed., pp. 222 (Birkhäuser Verlag, Basel, 1987).

25 Ronner, H.; Jhaveri, S.: Complete Work 1935 – 74; 2nd ed., pp. 293 (Birkhäuser Verlag, Basel, 1987).

26 Wurman, R.S.: What will be has always been. The words of Louis I. Kahn; comments on the library, Phillips Exeter Academy, Exeter, 1972; pp. 179 (Access Press / Rizzoli, New York, 1986).

27 Wurman, R.S.: What will be has always been. The words of Louis I. Kahn; comments on the library, Phillips Exeter Academy, Exeter, 1972; pp. 180 (Access Press / Rizzoli, New York, 1986).

28 Wurman, R.S.: What will be has always been. The words of Louis I. Kahn; comments on the library, Phillips Exeter Academy, Exeter, 1972; pp. 130 (Access Press / Rizzoli, New York, 1986).

29 Louis I. Kahn and the Kimbell Art Museum: Light is the theme; comments on architecture by Louis I. Kahn; pp. 33 (Kimbell Art Foundation, Fort Worth, Tex., 1975).

30 Ronner, H.; Jhaveri, S.: Complete Work 1935 – 74; 2nd ed., pp. 345 (Birkhäuser Verlag, Basel, 1987).

31 Wurman, R.S.: What will be has always been. The words of Louis I. Kahn; comments on the library, Phillips Exeter Academy, Exeter, 1972; pp. 216 (Access Press / Rizzoli, New York, 1986).

32 Ronner, H.; Jhaveri, S.: Complete Work 1935 – 74; 2nd ed., pp. 365 (Birkhäuser Verlag, Basel, 1987).

33 Ronner, H.; Jhaveri, S.: Complete Work 1935 – 74; 2nd ed., pp. 363 (Birkhäuser Verlag, Basel, 1987).

34 Ronner, H.; Jhaveri, S.: Complete Work 1935 – 74; 2nd ed., pp. 234 (Birkhäuser Verlag, Basel, 1987).

35 Ronner, H.; Jhaveri, S.: Complete Work 1935 – 74; 2nd ed., pp. 238 (Birkhäuser Verlag, Basel, 1987).

36 Ronner, H.; Jhaveri, S.: Complete Work 1935 – 74; 2nd ed., pp. 239 (Birkhäuser Verlag, Basel, 1987).

37 Ronner, H.; Jhaveri, S.: Complete Work 1935 – 74; 2nd ed., pp. 257 (Birkhäuser Verlag, Basel, 1987).

David B. Brown Lee, David G. De Long; Louis I. Kahn, in the Realm of Architecture, introduction by Vincent Scully. Rizzoli International Publications, Inc., New York, NY 1991: 13. W. Christensen; Scale Models and Molds, Philadelphia PA: 104 br.

R. Girgula, J. Metha; Louis I. Kahn. Verlag fÅr Architektur, Artemis Verlag, Zurich and Munich 1978: 87, 94 a, 104, 108, 110 bl, 149 l, 176 a, Il Parlamento e la Nuova Capitale a Dacca di Louis I. Kahn, 1962-74. Officina Edizioni, Rome 1985: 171 br. August E. Komendant; 18 Years with Architect Louis I. Kahn. Aloray Publisher, Englewood, NJ 1975: 84 bl. Alessandra Latour; Louis I. Kahn, Writings, Lectures, Interviews. Rizzoli International Publications, Inc., New York, NY: 186. J.D. Prown; The Architecture of the Yale Center for British Art, Yale University, New Haven, CN 1977: 1148. H. Ronner, S. Jhaveri and Institute for History and Theory of Architecture ETH Zurich; Louis I. Kahn, Complete Work 1935-1974. BirkhÑuser Basel, Boston 1977, 1987: 41, 60, 61, b, 64 ar br, 66 r, 67, 69, 70 ar bl, 74, 75 br, 79, 80, 81, 84 a br, 86 al, 88, bl, 89, 90, 91, 94 bl b, 98 a, 100, 101, 102 br, 105 al, 112 bl r, 113 l br, 116 a, 117, 121 br, 124 ar br, 128 bl, 132 a, 135 br, 137 br, 142 ar br, 146 bl, 156 al ar, 158 bl. Vincent Scully Jr.; Louis I. Kahn, Nr. 2. George Braziller, Inc., New York, NY 1962; 40. Richard Saul Wurman; What will be has always been. The Words of Louis I. Kahn. Access Press Ltd. and Rizzoli International Publications, Inc., New York, NY 1986: 11, 15, 17. Louis I. Kahn, Conception and Meaning. Architecture and Urbanism, Tokyo, November 1983; 122 r.

Louis Kahn - Tourisme - ActualitÇs. L'Architecture d'Aujourd'hui, Bologna (Seine), France, January 1963: 75 l, 76 b, 104 a, 105 ar br, 119. Louis I. Kahn 1901-74. Rassegna 21, Bologna, March 1979: 111 br.

Light is the Theme, Louis I. Kahn and the Kimbell Art Museum, Comments on Architecture by Louis . Kahn. Compiled by Nell E. Johnson, Kimbell Art Foundation, Fort Worth, TX 1975: 134, 135 l. Louis I. Kahn Collection. University of Pennsylvania and Pennsylvania Historical and Museum Commission, Philadelphia, PA: 31 al, 38 al ar bl br, 46 r, 48, 50 a b, 52, 53, 54 r, 56, 58 ar, 62 r, 68, 72 al ar b, 78, 86 ar, 88 r, 105 bl, 116 b, 118, 136, 137 l, 146 al, 150, 152 a br. The National Assembly Building, Dhaka, Department of Architecture and Public Government of the People's Republic of Bartgladesh 1984: 160, 162.

Urs Büttiker, Basel, Switzerland; 17, 19, 21, 23, 25, 27, 29, 31 ar bl br, 33, 33, 35, 36, 37, 39, 41, 43, 44, 45, 46 bl, 47, 49, 51, 54 bl, 45, 47, 48 al br, 49, 61 a, 62 bl, 63, 64 l, 65, 66 bl m, 70 br, 71, 73, 76 a, 77, 82, 83, 85, 86 b, 92, 93, 95, 96, 97, 98 bl br, 99, 102 bl ar, 103, 106, 107, 110, 101 ar, 112, 114, 115, 120, 121 l, 130 bl, 123, 124 bl, 126, 128, 127, 128 r, 130, 131, 132 b, 133, 138, 139, 140 bl r, 141, 142 bl, 146 ar br, 147, 149 r, 151 l, 154, 155, 156 bl br, 157, 158 a b, 159, 161, 163, 164, 165, 166, 167, 168, 169, 170, 171 l, 172, 173, 174 b, 175, 176, 175, 179, 180, 181. Eugen Eisenhut and Esther Zumsteg, Zurich, Switzerlnd; 129, 143, 144, 145. Gunar Volkmann, Lorrach, Germany: 151 br, 152 bl, 153, Esther Zumsteg, Zurich, Switzerland: 7.

I would like to extend my heartfelt appreciation here to all of those who helped me with this book. Its publication would not have been possible without the encouraging support which I received from many people.

Mrs. Julia Moore Converse at the Architectural Archives of the University of Pennsylvania provided help in the form of word and deed. I am particularly grateful to Werner Blaser, who invited me to a lecture on Louis I. Kahn at the Kunsthalle in Basel. It was this lecture which inspired me to compile my collected information in book form. Hans-Peter Thür of Birkhäuser Publishers generously granted me time, understanding, and trust during the long effort with my book. Without the support of Martina Düttmann in Berlin, who collaborated on the layout and edited the text, it would not have been possible to finish the book. David Bean translated the text into English. Heinz Hiltbrunner designed the cover.

Heartfelt thanks also go to Esther Zumsteg and to Hans-Jörg Tschäni, who both enthusiastically and carefully helped to revise the layout, and who produced the emblems and the technical drawings.

In the USA, India, Bangladesh, and here in Switzerland, I met many people who have generously provided information on Louis I. Kahn and his architecture. I would also like to extend my thanks to all of them at this point.